Slicing Heaven

Slicing Heaven

Tales, Poetry, and Recipes from
The Slice of Heaven
24-Hour Pie Shop and Driving Range

by
Barbara Jean Walsh

The material included in this book has been excerpted from the "Slice of Heaven" blog written by Barbara Jean Walsh. You may visit it online at http://slicingheaven.com/original

First Printing
January 2014

Sunshine Arts & Letters
1711 Santa Clara Ave.
Alameda, California 94501

© Barbara Jean Walsh 2014

Contents

Foreword	9
Golf Lesson Number One	11
September Full Moon	12
Another Golf Lesson	14
Poetry and Coffee (Sorry, No Pie)	15
Lemonade Pie	16
Golf Tip Number Four	17
Evolution or Creation?: The Story of Eggs Benedict Pie	19
Peeled Onion Dream Pie	21
Sometimes You Can Get Enough . . . of Barry White	23
Spawn of Satan Pie	26
Spawn of Satan Pie Recipe	31
After the Fall Pie	32
Perfect Timing	35
Rain and Reading	38
The Heart of Saturday Night	41
Nassau Airport Day Four	43
What Do You Do?	45
Tale of a Pink Hat	46
Full Moon, Clouds, and Wind (Part Two)	49
The Best Photos are the Ones I Never Took	51
But You Look So Cuban	53
Chocolate Cuban-Rum Pie	56
My Map of Havana	58
Karaoke Golf	60
Fried Steak in Space	62

The Things That They Took	64
Museums: Pie and Revolution	68
Pumpkin Cheesecake Pie	73
The Philosopher Detective	75
Hollywood Halloween	79
Your Second-Cousin Darnell and the Goat	84
Eating Humble Pie	88
Humble Pie Recipe	91
Yoga Retreat Golf Meditation	92
Four and Twenty Blackbirds	94
Michel Ten	96
The Caddy	100
Will Work for Pie	104
Chocolate-Laced Lemon Chiffon Pie	108
Full Moon Ramble	110
Night Golf Flu Shot Clinic	112
Mississippi	115
Cinderella's Pumpkin Pie	119
I Am Not My Brother's Driver	121
The *Cosmo* Quiz	123
When Clowns Play Golf	125
Sweet Potato-Clock Pie!	128
Elbow Room	132
Zombie Golf	134
A New Year	136
Key Lime Pie: The Search Begins	139
Whole Earth Everything, Now on The Pie Shop Shelves	142
Key Lime Pie Test (Rusty Pelican, Biscayne Bay, Florida)	144
National Pie Day Eve	146
A Couple More Slices of Key Lime Pie	148
String Theory Pie	150

Looking for Golf in All the Wrong Places	151
Intergalactic Sports	154
Go Cry on Somebody Else's Shoulder	155
The Gimme	158
Steampunk Cafe	160
Get a Grip	162
An Urgency of Pay Phones	164
Spring Training	168
On the Other Side of the Edge of the 'Glades	171
Sundial for Little Peach	174
Linton and Swinton and Michigan	175
Swing Thoughts Poem	178
National Pie Championships (Part Two)	180
You Got to Have Friends	182
In Hot Pursuit of Happiness	185
Why I Live at the Sand Trap	189
Muffins	191
Lemon Mirage Pie	193
The City	196
Moon Landing	199
Taxi Driver	201
Pie Poems for the Poetry Pie	204
The Line	207
Ethan Coen's Poem	209
The Winds of Insomnia	212

Foreword

At the end of the first decade of the current century, most Americans were filled with questions about Barack Obama's fledgling administration, the economy, and foreign policy.

At The Slice of Heaven 24-Hour Pie Shop and Driving Range, though, we tended to set those concerns aside lest they interfere with our search for the ultimate slice of Key lime pie, our hopes that the ringing pay phone would be a call from you, and the fantasy that our missing luggage would finally return from Havana.

And, of course, we never stopped believing that some day every single one of us would experience true perfection in the form of an absolutely authentic golf swing.

I haven't been back there for a while myself, but if you drop in, please say "Hello" to everyone for me. I miss them all more every day, and I just can't wait until we can all spend some time together on the edge of the 'Glades once again.

Barbara Jean Walsh
Alameda, California
January 2014

Golf Lesson Number One

The Morning Guy gave me a golf lesson—by email—a couple of weeks ago. I was hoping for something more personal, like the snuggly stuff they always show in the movies, but I will take what I can get.

As it turns out, I am doing most of this anyway, but maybe I am not doing it right.

Here goes: "Golf lesson number one: At the range, take time in between every hit. After the hit, step away from the next ball. Think of how you just hit the ball. Think of the feeling of hitting. Regrip correctly. Step up to the ball correctly. And hit the next ball. Repeat."

You see, it's all Zen. I love this game.

September Full Moon

I went out to the driving range earlier than I had planned because I was a little worried about the usual weather prediction of thunder storms, but then I live in SoFLA so what do I expect? Still I did not want to get shut out, so I had my 100 balls ready to go long before the full moon came up at 7:30.

After no practice for more than a week, I didn't feel much flow, and that's probably much of what I will feel in tomorrow's Ashtanga yoga class, too.

The lighting tonight was exquisite. I wished I had grabbed my camera, thinking that the sky I was seeing would be just perfect on the ceiling of The Pie Shop, oh hell, puffy clouds turning all pink and gold against an impossibly blue background. Just the sort of thing I would have drawn in third grade and been told, as I was, that it was unrealistic.

The sky to the west, though, was steel gray, and foreboding. No matter. It was all bluff, no action.

At first there was a lot of chatter, lessons taking place, tips being offered, ah, but not for me.

I settled in for an evening of way too many swings and misses, marveling at how many little things go into a righteous hit, worrying about the recent misses elsewhere in my life, trying not to get too spaced out on metaphors.

Yes, yes, yes, I want to believe that golf is all Zen, but then I'm noting, too, my check list of motions and notions. I hear the guy behind me advising his friend to separate the new bright yellow balls from the old faded ones and see what difference that makes.

Oh, no! I am not ready for that level of refinement.

What I want first is consistency. I just want to see if I can repeat the few good strong hits that please me so much. It seems that I am setting up the same every time, but apparently not. Some piece is missing. I try putting different thoughts in my head. I get engrossed in my imagination and my body goes ahead with the swing.

Meanwhile my right toes, all five of them, are cramping up and that does a lot to help with focus now, doesn't it? I sing a little to myself. The guy next to me swears, not about the singing. At least I don't think so. Then, when I see that I am running low on balls, I start to feel sad because I will be done.

No great breakthrough or giant step ahead tonight, but a satisfying practice. I know from swimming and yoga that the tiny improvements will continue to add up, and it will all come down to learning to breathe, and that has been the story of my life for the past five years.

Or, as John Lennon once said, "As breathing is my life, to stop I dare not dare."

Another Golf Lesson

I love how almost everything I am learning about golf is a life lesson. Consequently, I am in no hurry ever to get beyond the driving range and on to the course.

This morning, my golf instructor Sandra at the Country Club in The Village and I spent an hour pretty much just on alignment and relaxing. "You want to feel like you have a buzz on." Oh, yes. There's a goal I can appreciate.

Slow down, slow down, slow down.

Then finally I hit one and don't feel it at all. The ball just flies away, not far, but straight. We smile. We nod.

"Excellent," she says, and I hit five in a row. I am psyched and happy.

She changes my grip into one that seems awkward at first, but works so well that I am sold in a matter of minutes.

The alignment lesson may have been easier for many people, but I already know from yoga with The Yoga Guy that I have little sense of alignment, and I need to trust someone else's judgment on that. What feels lined up to me apparently does not meet the classic definition, but I can learn the steps to the dance.

And I shall.

Poetry and Coffee (Sorry, No Pie)

The Morning Guy claims not to listen to NPR, but he does seem to read Garrison Keillor's website "The Writer's Almanac" which astounds and confuses me. I do listen to NPR, but built up a sensitivity to Keillor's voice over the years until it has become a sound akin to fingernails on a blackboard. But that's another story.

At any rate, I was surprised to find this poem—"Literature in the 21st Century" by Ronald Wallace—in my in-box this morning, before I even thought about starting to work. "Everyone must read poetry with their coffee," The Morning Guy had written on the attached sea-blue Post-It note. I'm not sure if that is meant to be a new rule—he has many of those—or just an observation.

Sadly for me, like the narrator of the poem, I no longer drink coffee. Or smoke. Or drink. Damn, sometimes life is hard. No wonder I look forward to those stormy days when Hurricane Rules apply. I used to love a shot of 100-proof Hot Damn followed by a beer chaser. Oddly enough, I just don't get the same kick from a cinnamon Altoid and an O'Doul's.

And I do miss drinking coffee with my poetry. At least I'll always have pie.

Lemonade Pie

Didn't get what I wanted, and you know what they said? "Honey, when life hands you a lemon, make lemonade." I always said, "When life hands you a lemon, look for tequila and salt."

How to make Lemonade Pie

    Take all your disappointments, sorrows, and, grievances
    Soak in tequila overnight
    Wake up wanting something sweet and crunchy
    Find it
    Mash it up for the crust with real butter
    And extra cinnamon
    Distill the liquid ingredients
    Until you have something you can use
    Fold in some whole organic eggs and heat ever so slowly
    In time it will thicken
    In time it will jell
    Pour into the crust
    And then, baby,
    All you need to do is
    Chill

Golf Tip Number Four

A couple of days ago, The Morning Guy gave me another tip. It took him three Post-Its to write it all out. Fortunately, he has very precise and legible handwriting:

"You are ready for golf tip Number Four," he writes. "The ball should be aligned the same place in relation to your left heel every time. The driver's ball should be aligned inside the left heel. The wedge's ball should be aligned equidistant between the two heels. Never go to the right of that spot. All other clubs should be aligned on a line from the driver to the wedge depending on the club length."

I do not have a clue about what he is telling me, and I scribble a note, wanting to know what happened to Tip Number Two and Tip Number Three. Then when I got to work this morning, I found his answer on a napkin taped to my inbox: "They are grip tips and are better taught by showing not by words."

Obviously, I will need someone else to teach me grip tips since The Morning Guy has successfully avoided having to deal with me in person for months, and he is unlikely to change any time soon.

And yet, we do stay in touch. It's a reliable relationship, not a satisfying one. I know I am not ready for Golf Tip Number Four. It has way too many variations, so I will just stick with the changes that Sandra gave me at my last lesson. And I will practice, practice, practice.

Last night, I admit, I did get sucked into that color thing. Yes, I saved the shiny yellow ones until the last, and I swear it made a difference. Better balls? Is that what it's all about? Better sticks? Finer tools. What about sheer skill and determination? Maybe I should stick to swimming, but no. I love the color, sounds, and smell of the whole thing too much. I'll just work on style for now and worry about new equipment later on.

I will note, though, that I'm tempted to post a new rule out on the range: "No Married Couples Allowed." A little harsh? Maybe. But I just don't enjoy being that close to non-communicating people. If I wanted to hear bickering, I would still be living at Lake of the Ozarks watching men trying to direct their wives in backing their trailer-boats down the ramp.

On the other hand, I did love seeing a dad & a pre-teen daughter hanging out together. They can come back and play for free. Anytime. We're open 24-hours a day.

Evolution or Creation?: The Story of Eggs Benedict Pie

In 1894, the story goes, Lemmy Benedict, bored and hungover, told the chef at the Waldorf Astoria that he wanted something different for breakfast.

What he ordered doesn't seem all that different: poached eggs, bacon, and buttered toast. But he also asked for a pitcher of hollandaise sauce and proceeded to build his own treat.

The chef, Oscar Tschirky, later made his own variation, and put it on the menu with English muffins and sauteed ham, but Lemmy never approved of Oscar's version. No, the real deal was the way Lemmy made it and that was that.

The history of Eggs Benedict is now more than 100 years old, and although a lot of people have taken a whack at creating the E. B., but like so many things in life, all they can do is build on the original idea, the one where Lemmy Benedict ordered up that pitcher of sauce.

Toast or muffins? Toast or artichoke hearts? Salmon instead of ham? I'd be willing to try any of them, especially if I were at the Waldorf Astoria with a hangover.

Here, at The Slice of Heaven 24-hour Pie Shop and Driving Range, we have our own delectable version of Lemmy's dish: Eggs Benedict Pie.

We make it in an individual serving dish with a breadcrumb crust, baked with brushed butter, topped with piping hot Canadian bacon, two poached eggs, and as much hollandaise sauce as you can stand, garnished with one of those cute little sprigs of parsley, just for a touch of color, and a sprinkling of paprika.

If we served liquor, we'd give you a Bloody Mary, too, but we don't, so you'll have to settle for our trademarked Bloody Shame. But if you slip in a bit of something from your own hip flask, we won't try to stop you.

Want to go the vegetarian route? We are willing to negotiate. Just remember. At The Slice of Heaven 24-hour Pie Shop and Driving Range, we use only real ingredients.

Peeled Onion Dream Pie

"Just peel the onion," they say.
"Peel back the layers
and see what you find."

I say "Nothing,"
but I am wrong.

Nothing is just what I found
at the time,
but now I know it's full of space,
and space of course is full of stars.

So we talk about observation,
seeing time move, and
wondering when and how
simple viewing
moved its way
through the amygdala
to turn itself into critical thinking.

To make this pie,
I suggest you start with
just one large,
unfathomably sweet
Vidalia onion.

Peel it back

until all you can see is
stars, motion,
and mathematics.

Opine to your heart's desire.

Percolate.

Steep overnight.

Reflect and finally
inject with just enough emotion
to give it that special zip.

Spread over a thick skin
of bread dough and minced onion.

Bake in a wood-fired adobe oven
in the dark heart of night
just north of Nogales
while you sing with coyotes
and breathe in the same stars
that you formerly
could not see inside the onion.

Serve in a paper bag.

Try to think your way out of it.

Sometimes You Can Get Enough . . . of Barry White

Last night, out on the driving range, well after dark, I go through 100 balls in only an hour, which I know is much too fast.

I'm not spending enough time in the silent space between the swings, and I'm going too fast when I am swinging, so I know I need to adjust my sense of time and timing and slow it all right down.

As usual, I need to find a source for the defect, and so today I am passing the blame on to Wendy's Chocolate-Chip Cookie Dough Frosty, a 480-calorie treat, and 25% of those calories are from fat. W00t!

The "healthy alternatives" website suggests that I would have been wiser to go for the Mandarin Chicken Salad instead, but it's just not the same kick, and standing around with a Mandarin Chicken Salad would not endear me to the local golf teens as much as the Chocolate-Chip Cookie Dough Frosty does.

"Wow," says one bright-eyed local boy. "I just had one of those two hours ago, and I am still buzzing." My point exactly. If I'd gotten mine with chocolate ice cream instead of just chocolate-chip, I would probably still be out there.

Then again, I didn't sleep well, and I am out there again at 7:00 a.m., hitting balls and musing about the events of the past nine or so hours. Picture me now driving too fast on I-95, high on way too much sugar but happily reviewing the evening's progress, remembering the voices of the two men next to me, softly sharing advice and stories, whistling low in appreciation as one or the other hits a truly spectacular shot.

I am happy. I am cruising on the super-highway that can be seen from space, and I am listening to jazz and thinking about The Morning Guy who is out somewhere for his evening run, staying fit, keeping the boxes in his mind all nicely organized and never letting them touch each other, and then it happens: The radio inexplicably switches from jazz to Barry White, and I hear Barry moaning about how he cannot get enough of my love.

Suddenly, my mood goes from crest-of-the-wave to serious paper cut, and I feel like I just plunged my hand into a vat of organic lemon juice. I want to swerve into the nearest bar and knock back some Jack Daniels Black to ward off the unexpected and unwelcome stab of loneliness.

For just a split second, I even find myself missing my two ex-husbands Pretty Boy Boyd and Patrick-the-Liar, but that impulse blinks out of existence just as quickly as a firefly being eaten by a bat.

The next song, though, is equally devastating, and I am plotting the shortest route to Pepe's Hideaway, when my cell phone jangles, and it is Sue Ten, stranded at a Starbucks with a folding bike and no interest in pedaling any farther.

"I was just reaching out for a human connection," she says. Relieved to have a diversion, I say I understand fully, and continue south, well past my exit, slowing down to navigate a major speed trap, where there are at least a dozen blue lights flashing. I pick her up in a matter of minutes.

On the way to her deluxe double-wide, we debate The Pie Shop menu. I am not at all convinced that her version of Eggs Benedict Pie, with sliced potatoes instead of a crust, works for me.

She argues for more variety in the menu. I'm holding my ground. I'm running a 24-Hour Pie Shop and Driving Range, not a cafe. And I like purity of definition. What's she's offering is a casserole. I will only serve pie and metaphors.

So this message is for all of you who want more than what I have to offer: Get in your pick-up truck and just go next door to The Swing Barn. You can talk to Sue Ten, in Italian no less, and you can eat whatever you like. You can even have waffle fries covered with cheese-in-a-can. You can swing dance. You can weep in your beer.

Remember, though, The Swing Barn is not open 24-hours a day, there's no free internet, and there aren't even any good books to read. Although some of the graffiti in the rest rooms—which, by the way, have signs saying "Them" and "Us" on the doors—is pretty interesting.

Now, if you want a pie for dessert, give us a call, and I'll send Joe Sparkle Junior over in a golf cart to deliver it to you. Please have exact change.

Life can be so easy.

Spawn of Satan Pie

I'm out on the driving range before noon today, but I can't concentrate. Today, I will blame the New York Yankees since their fans are coming out of the woodwork to mourn the passing of their blessed temple in the Bronx.

All my hits are off kilter, low, and lethargic, obviously affected by all that negative energy. In time, I give up and go back into The Pie Shop, to get out of the heat as much as anything.

I take out my notepad and start working on a recipe for "Spawn of Satan Pie" with a special Derek Jeter Crust. Jeter's favorite food is Chicken Parmesan, so this is a no brainer, and I know I'll be getting calls from Sue Ten over at The Swing Barn once the pre-game show starts at six.

It's one of those hot, humid SoFLA days that keeps people indoors, so I'm not expecting much excitement today. I gave The Usual Idiot the day off, and I'm thinking this might be a good time to varnish the new combination step-ladder bookshelves out in the back room, with the exhaust fan going full blast.

The Morning Guy copied the design that I found last week, and he's already built the prototype, finished the sanding, and vacuumed up every stray bit of sawdust. He'll be leaving me snitty notes if I don't get moving on this project soon.

I like varnishing, especially roll-and-tip with warm varnish. It goes on fast, the tipping with a foam brush breaks down the bubbles, and then I can just pull up a chair and watch it dry. In truth, it's more fun to watch it dry if someone else did the application work, but I know I'll see plenty: curtains, holidays, bugs in their death throes, visions of alternate universes, dreams of another time and place. It's all entertainment to the receptive mind. Varnish, sand, repeat. Shampoo, rinse, repeat. Signs of infinity in the known universe.

I'm sure, too, that the sound of the fan will drown out the noise from the over-emotional Yankees fans at The Swing Barn. If not, I have a set of Ruger firing-range ear muffs that should do the job.

Before I can put them on, though, the phone rings. It's Sue Ten. "Boyd's here."

"I wondered why Hercules was heading that way."

Hercules is our resident feral green iguana, a gargantuan beast by all accounts, and for some reason, he has an attraction for my second ex-husband Pretty Boy Boyd. Hercules' affection, however, is not returned. Boyd has a deep abiding dislike of all things reptilian, including his own lizard brain.

I look out the window and see my old car in the far side of the parking lot. A lime green Toyota Celica, it was a parting gift, or bribe. It was the WD-40 that lubricated the hinges of the exit-only door that Boyd finally opened.

"What's he up to?" I ask Sue.

"He's pretty quiet so far," says Sue. "Not annoying anyone too much. Just the usual ranting about The Royals and how many players started out in Kansas City. Apparently, he no longer has a television at home."

"And what's he calling home these days?"

"Hard to tell," says Sue. "A couple more drinks, and I'm sure I'll have his full life story. Again."

"Sorry, honey, but he's your customer," I say. "The restraining order has expired. Give him some waffle fries on the house. If he's busy eating, he won't be able to talk as much."

I'm rattled, but I go back to varnishing anyway. Roll. Tip. Roll. Tip. One. Two. Lift. Swing. Lift. Swing. I'm reviewing this morning's practice, more convinced than ever that negative Yankees energy was my enemy, and Boyd was all too often a fan of The Best Team That Money Can Buy.

I had not watched baseball for years when I met him, but he awoke something deep and significant in me: A Red Sox fan's utter hatred of the New York Yankees, and it felt good for me to know an emotion that deep and pure. Yes! It's the opposite end of the mood-spectrum from that mystifying ability that some people have that allows them to say, in any situation, "It's all good."

Anti-Yankeeism consists of a certitude and clarity of vision found primarily in extreme religious sects, and it's a wonderfully cleansing experience. I do recommend it.

Boyd was never much of a golf fan, though. So, now I can picture him at the bar, telling his usual two golf jokes. "Oh, yes," he says, "I agree with Mark Twain that golf is a good walk spoilt." Not that he'd know what a good walk is either.

And when someone asks him if he plays, he say, "I do. I love golf, but I always have trouble getting the ball through the windmill and into the clown's mouth."

By now he is telling Sue his one remaining joke. "You know why a bartender is like a priest?"

I can see the beatific look of unbearable patience on her face now, her chin cocked to the side, her hand smoothly reaching for the taser under the counter.

She doesn't answer, just raises her eyebrows a bit in a questioning glance.

"They both serve wine and take confessions," says Boyd, laughing too loud. The rest of the bar goes silent, except for Madeleine Peyroux on the jukebox singing

"I'm All Right." Maybe even singing my favorite line, "Wherever you are, you're still driving my car."

As I hear it later, Hercules has planted himself directly behind Boyd's bar stool and has nudged off one of Boyd's baby-blue flip-flops. The hush continues as everyone but Boyd, happily oblivious, watches the iguana chomp down on one all too tempting big left toe.

Boyd's already pale skin goes white, and then he screams, looks down, sees Hercules, and screams again.

"Now, now," says Sue. "I believe you are supposed to remain calm in situations like this. Can you do that, Boyd?"

He nods, thin-lipped, eyes clamped shut. Sue pats his hand and flashes that beatific smile again.

"Now, my understanding is that we need to turn this sucker upside down to get him to release you. Ready?"

She motions to a couple of the regulars, one in a Yankees tee-shirt and the other in a faded-orange Orioles shirt. They pick up Hercules and twist him, and Boyd's toe in the process, with no positive results.

"What about the alcohol trick?" Sue asks.

"Okay," says the Oriole's fan. He picks up Boyd's schooner of Guinness and pours it over Boyd's foot and Hercules' face. The well-fed iguana still does not budge.

"Only one more thing to do," says Sue. "Load them both up and get them to the emergency room." She points to the door.

"I can't do that," says Boyd.

"Oh yes you can," says Sue. "It's either that, lose your toe, or spend the rest of your life with an iguana attached to your foot."

She gives the two good Samaritans a quick hand signal and twenty dollars, and they load up Boyd and

Hercules, dropping them both in the back of a blue Chevy pick-up truck.

I look out the window just in time to glimpse a truck take off down the hot and dusty road. Sue is already on the phone giving me the delicious details. I tell her I saw Boyd in the back of truck and his long white ponytail had come undone.

"By the time they reach the hospital, he will have a serious case of uncombable hair syndrome," I say, "Not to mention the more obvious foot-in-iguana-mouth condition."

"Yes, it's sad," she says.

I notice, as we talk, that there's a little activity going on by the back door of The Swing Barn. Usually, Sue keeps that door shut tight to minimize uninvited guests, such as large feral green iguanas.

I'm about to tell her I'm surprised to see the back door open, and then I see The Morning Guy, laughing to himself, closing the door and walking away. No need to mention that to anyone.

And it's time for me to bake some chicken-parmesan pie before the game gets underway.

Spawn of Satan Pie Recipe

Created in honor of New York Yankee Derek Jeter's birthday

INGREDIENTS

3/4 cup ricotta cheese
1/3 cup grated Parmesan cheese
1 1/2 cup cut-up cooked chicken
1 1/4 cup shredded Mozzarella cheese
1 clove garlic, minced
2 t fresh chopped oregano
2 t fresh basil
6-oz tomato paste
1 cup heavy cream
2 large eggs
2/3 cup Bisquick
Salt and pepper to taste

DIRECTIONS

Pre-heat oven to 400 degrees F.

Grease a 10-inch by 1-1/2-inch pie plate with butter.

Alternate layers of Ricotta cheese and Parmesan cheese.

Mix chicken, 1/2 C Mozzarella, garlic powder, oregano, basil, and tomato paste.

Pour over Parmesan cheese layer.

Whisk together cream, eggs, Bisquick, salt & pepper.

Pour into pie plate.

Bake 30 minutes.

Top with remaining Mozzarella.

Bake an addition five to 10 minutes, or until toothpick inserted in center comes out clean.

After the Fall Pie

"Don't forget, it's the first day of fall," my sister Melbie tells me on the phone. As I hear her voice, I am sure she is wearing at least one sweater and knows where her boots are. After all, that's basic survival behavior in the Great State of Maine.

I, too, know that it's fall, even here in SoFLA: The traffic on I-95 is starting to pick up, the sidewalk cafes in the village are bustling again, and the boutiques are showing pink sweaters with fur trim.

And out at The Slice of Heaven 24-Hour Pie Shop and Driving Range, we are on the look out for migrating birds and we're starting to get orders for apple pie, pumpkin pie, and squash pie. One more month, and the mince-pie people will be showing up.

There are other signs of fall, too: The ubiquitous football games on every flat screen in every bar, the faux fall leaves in the shop windows, and the Halloween decorations already up in the Winn-Dixie.

As I talk to Melbie, the idea for an "After the Fall" pie pops into my mind: It should have both apples and pomegranates to signify the mixed myths of Adam and Eve and Persephone.

No doubt at all: Pomegranate is a powerful fruit, a particular favorite of the lords of the underworld, which would of course include Satan. I think it's too bad for the lovely, innocuous apple to take the rap for The Fall of Humankind. Mythologists feel it was much more likely caused by Eve's consumption of pomegranates—and possibly a whole lot of wine.

Persephone also had a pomegranate problem. If she'd never been tricked into eating those seeds, we'd have summer all year round. Oh, wait a minute. I live in SoFLA. We do have summer all year round.

I'm still thinking about my After the Fall pie, not sure where to go with it. I take a break and put on my CD of the Pogues singing "If I Should Fall from Grace with God," but it is so jarring that I can't listen to the whole song.

I'm also thinking about the movie *After the Fall*, in which Brad Pitt inexplicably never ages, although the rest of the cast appears to be quite gnarly by the end.

After that, I come up with the idea that Eve didn't just eat an apple. Or a pomegranate. I don't think it was wine either. No, I'm pretty sure she got into the applejack. Now, if you've never sampled applejack, this may not be the time to start.

My oh my.

Consumed with the right amount of gusto on a crisp fall night, possibly over on the other side of The Swing Barn where Sue Ten has those cute little hard-resin chairs with cup holders, applejack will remove the top of your head and fill your brain with autumn leaves.

So, I'll just give you a little taste.

AFTER THE FALL PIE RECIPE

First, buy a large bottle of applejack brandy, and prepare your favorite type of unbaked crust with fluted edges. *Maybe make the pie crust first.*

A 9-in pie plate should be just about right.

For the filling

Peel & slice six tart apples

Soak apple slices in a cup of applejack brandy

overnight, and maybe take a sip or two yourself, just to make sure it's all right.

In the morning, cream 4oz of butter with 8oz of sugar.

When the mixture is light and fluffy, strain the apples and fold them in.

A little lemon zest wouldn't hurt.

How's that brandy, anyway?

Cover with foil and bake at 400 degrees for 30 minutes.

Feel free to have another drink while you wait, or go ahead and make the topping.

For the topping

Cover the hot apple mixture with a layer of thin pomegranate slices.

Whip a cup of heavy cream, then blend in 3 to 4 T of sugar and 3 egg yolks .

Cover the pomegranate slices with the whipped topping and return to the oven for 10 minutes, or until topping is golden brown.

Garnish with pomegranate seeds.

Drizzle any remaining applejack over all.

Chances are, the applejack will have disappeared by the time you get to this step.

And just like Adam & Eve, you should probably go put some clothes on, too.

Perfect Timing

I've never been someone known for her timing, or at least not for her good timing. Pretty Boy Boyd, my second ex-husband, used to tell me at least once a week, "Your timing stinks." Of course, that retort would usually come right after my weekly suggestion that he find a new place to live. And yet, tonight, my timing is so good that I go through 97 golf balls before the rain starts. And hitting those last three in rain is a pleasure.

After all, I've already had more than solid hour of practice, and during most of that time, my young employee Joe Sparkle Junior is out on the tractor, scooping up balls. I've got to say, I've never seen anyone operate a tractor quite so slowly or carefully, and it surprises me, since Sparkle Junior is usually pretty wound up on sugar and caffeine. I suspect that The Morning Guy may have had a word with him at some point about safety, responsibility, and keeping his job.

So, Sparkle Junior is making his transit, carefully and endlessly, and the late night crowd is, as usual, entrancing me with their high and long arcs. I definitely prefer to practice at night under the lights so I can watch the balls, and tonight we've got some good hits going on, even without the metallic clang of New Age drivers.

Behind me there is an Asian guy, who is so obsessed with perfection that he continues to stand and work on his swing, long after his bucket is empty. I go over and speak to him for a second, just to make sure he understands that we do now have an "All You Can Hit" policy at The Slice of Heaven 24-Hour Pie Shop and Driving Range.

For some reason, he looks at me as if I am crazy and goes right on swinging at air. Apparently, he feels he's already gotten his money's worth. Myself, I would keep going until I can't go no more, but the rain ends that little reverie.

Speaking of our "All You Can Hit" policy, I had earlier imagined a sort of conveyor belt bringing the balls out to the range, but the engineering concept lost out to the K.I.S.S. Method, and I decided that people can just keep refilling their buckets. Too bad, though, I was looking forward to seeing what The Morning Guy would come up with to deliver the balls to the customers. Ah, well.

Tonight I'm getting in some nice swings, myself, but I'm uncomfortably aware that I am wearing the wrong bra. Something about this black underwire just isn't doing the trick for me. Then I think maybe I can use the aggravation to my advantage, like Tim Robbins wearing a garter belt in *Bull Durham*. Or maybe not.

I find myself longing for my favorite Body by Victoria orange bra, and make a mental note to look for more of the same type next time I'm at the mall, which is at best a twice a year event. Perhaps "the perfect golf bra" will offer The Morning Guy an even better engineering challenge, one that I am sure he can solve given the right data, parameters, and hypothetical situation.

I'm tempted to leave him a Post-It note, and maybe a catalog or two, but I resist: although, I do think he might secretly enjoy adding a lingerie subsection to his "proper attire" hints for golfers. Actually, I did conduct a quick internet search, and it appears that I may be the only one interested in finding the perfect golf bra anyway. Apparently, a number of people are looking for the perfect Volkswagen Golf bra, but that's not the same thing at all, now is it?

As I practice, I am again wondering about other kinds of equipment, too. I am still messing around with the same old nine-iron, and will do so until Sandra tells me to try something else.

"Your job is just to swing the club," she says, and I do. I look out at the target, then down at the ball, find my focus to the left, do some yogic hocus pocus, let my right hand pull up the club, and watch it drop down like a pendulum through my proposed path. If the ball is sitting in the right place to be hit, so much the better.

And all that time, the voice in my head is singing, "Don't mean a thing if you ain't got that swing, do wop do wop do wop do wah."

I'd write more, but I do have to get back to The Pie Shop. Sue Ten came by earlier to leave off something that she calls pie, but that I still say is a casserole. Back in Maine, there's an expression: "Just because a cat has kittens in the oven, that don't make them biscuits." And I feel the same way about pie: "Just because you throw some food into a round tin, that don't make it a pie."

Of course, this will probably just encourage her to bring over more possibilities. I sure hope so.

By the way, if you aren't doing anything on Friday night, you should stop by The Swing Barn. Sue was planning to show the McCain-Obama debate on her big-screen television, but now it looks like the debate won't be on, so she is going to show *Soylent Green* outside on the wall. Bring your own lawn chair and bug spray, but if you want a real pie, come see me.

And look, Sparkle Junior is finally bringing in the tractor. Perfect timing.

Rain and Reading

We're having a regular deluge here in SoFLA. Sue Ten reports that the IntraCoastal Waterway has overflowed, but the fisherfolk are still in place, with their aluminum folding chairs and bare feet just ever so slightly under water, and the snapper still biting.

The Pie Shop is having a busy morning. The lightning is keeping people off the range, so they come inside to eat pie instead, and they do admire our new step-stool bookshelves. I'm still stocking the shelves, carrying books down from the crawlspace where some of them have been stored for years.

When I was in the library trade, we had some basic rules for accepting book donations: If they've been stored in a basement or garage, forget it. If they've been in an attic, maybe. If they've been on "living shelves," go for it.

Books do better when they have a lot of human contact, and that's a big part of why I want to bring mine out and set them free.

I believe, very sincerely, that private ownership of books is counter-revolutionary, and books lose value when they are locked up. I always cringe a little when people show me their hordes of bookish treasure. I don't like it. I don't like it at all. Books die if they aren't handled and loved, and the best way to keep them healthy is to keep them moving.

Accordingly, this little collection in The Slice of Heaven 24-Hour Pie Shop and Driving Range will change pretty steadily as people find just the right thing to read, and as they take my books, they'll bring me the ones they've been keeping under grow lights in their own back rooms.

I've never worked in a library—or pie shop—where I didn't come out ahead on this kind of proposal.

I'm starting, of course, with some of my favorite golf stories—*The Legend of Bagger Vance*, *Golf in the Kingdom*, and even *Slim and None*, as soon as I'm done reading it. *Slim and None* is a Dan Jenkins' story, and although it's not as much fun as Jenkins' *Baja Oklahoma*, or as pithy as *Semi-Tough*, it does shine with that good old boy brand of humor. Taking that into consideration, I've got to wonder why I like it so much, but I do.

I rate Jenkins high as an entertaining writer, and I feel the same way about Peter Gent (*North Dallas 40*), and William Kinsella (whose *Shoeless Joe* later became *Field of Dreams*).

Personally, I find men to be the great mystery of life, and, although I do like chick-lit stories like Bridget Jones and the Shopaholic series, I have never especially enjoyed reading vaunted feminist writers. You see, I know how women think. That's easy.

But how men think? Now that is fascinating to me, and it's certainly easier to read about them than to have to go through the painful process of trying to get them to explain in their own words how and why they've chosen a particular path or made a specific decision.

My research on this subject has gone on for years, as I have sought clues in spy novels and crime novels and fiction by James Lee Burke, Michael Connelly, and John Grisham.

I like trashy books about men, and I like well-written books about men. I'm not ashamed to admit it at all. Sea stories? Pirate tales? Bring them on. Maybe I'll learn something new. Maybe I'll solve the puzzle and find eternal happiness. I am, if nothing else, an optimist.

All that aside, I'm sure our bookshelves will have no shortage of golf titles, or cook books. Those, I'm sure, will show up on their own. Myself, I'm bringing in a lot of paperback copies of William Faulkner, too, since I consider him and Henry James to be our greatest American writers.

I know a lot of the guys still think Ernie Hemingway is the best of the best, but really? Are they talking about his writing or his lifestyle? No, not for me. It's the Deep South of Faulkner that talks to me, and carries me into the kitchen to bake sweet-potato pie.

I've always liked to read about the South, and not just for the food. And not just Faulkner, but Flannery O'Connor, Eudora Welty, Walker Percy, and so many others. They offer a combination of lushness and decay, not unlike the vegetation that once encroached The Pie Shop's back door.

You know, I think building the driving range was one of the best things I ever did, just to clear the vines and god-damn night-blooming jasmine away from the back porch. I think it probably saved my life, or at least set me free, just the way that I like to set books free so they can breathe again.

Yes, the natural world is lovely, and all that, but these days I find the most intense beauty in the arc of the golf balls at night. And as soon as it stops raining, I'll grab a book or two and a big glass of lemonade, and head out to the back porch. Sparkle Junior is behind the counter serving pie, and if anyone wants to come out and practice, they can just hand me ten bucks for all the balls that they can hit.

No problem, no problem at all. I hope you'll join me soon.

The Heart of Saturday Night

I've been thinking about Darnell a lot lately. He's always seemed like family to me, even though he's your second cousin, not mine. I'm so glad that he moved back to SoFLA and got out of New York City, although it was always fun to hear the women on *The Montel Williams Show* talk about him, even though they never really had too much that was too good to say about him.

I guess what brings him to mind is that I keep hearing that Tom Waits song, "Looking for the Heart of Saturday Night," in my mind, and I love that one line, "Telephone's ringin'; it's your second cousin."

Yes, that would certainly be the heart of Saturday night here, or any other night for that matter. Darnell does a good job of looking out for all-you-all, especially now that he's found that elusive place called home.

Since Slice of Heaven is open 24-hours-a-day, I don't really have the sense of Saturday night that I once did, if I ever did. For me, it's always Friday night when I want to be out and about, and that's some of what drew me to the driving range part of my life. Fish and chips from The Swing Barn and an endless bucket of balls? What could be better than that?

I know I will look forward to spending some time out there this evening after the sun goes down. I hope I'll do better than I did on Monday, when almost every single shot was low and stupid. I mean, so low that some of them just jumped right back and bit my ankles.

I know I've been a little distracted lately, maybe overdue for a break from the usual routine, so you'll be glad to hear that my dear friend Little Peach and I are going to take ourselves on an adventure in about a week, when we head to Havana to celebrate my 60th birthday.

We've packed up our guidebooks and our comfy walking shoes, and we're ready to hear some new tunes. I don't know that I'll get to enjoy any golf there, but we are determined to come back with at least one new pie recipe, and I'll tell you all about it when we return.

In the meantime, though, I have a busy week to survive taking care of business in the city. I'll be leaving The Slice of Heaven in the capable hands of Sue Ten, The Morning Guy, and Sparkle Junior. I'd love to know if you are a Saturday night person, or a Friday night one like me. In either case, though, I hope you find the heart of it and it's just what you always wanted.

Nassau Airport Day Four

Just a fantasy, really. What if Little Peach and I never did get out of the Nassau Airport? And it did look like that for a while, but we are now safely ensconced in the Hotel Inglaterra on another island even farther south. We did have a small glitch checking in at the airport and that turned into a bigger glitch when our luggage did not arrive.

We had a difficult time telling Customs where we were planning to stay. They didn't buy our "Holiday Inn" answer, but we came up with another story. I am now probably well within the folklore of the airport: The woman who is celebrating her birthday with no luggage, but who gets on the next plane anyway.

Still in Nassau, though, we noticed a lot of pirate hoo-hah in the News Stand and immediately started thinking in terms of pie pirates, and even paw paw pirate pie. We think that pirates might like a salty crust, ho ho.

I learned that Little Peach, when young, had recurring dreams about monkeys. No monkey pie for her.

We also wondered about what might go into an Island Time Pie. We believe it might be the type of pie that is hard to get started on. It might be the kind of pie you eat when your know you want dessert, but maybe just not yet.

We also discussed the "While You Wait Pie"—some of you may remember my previous scheme for creating and selling "While You Wait" kits for stranded travelers (Little Peach & I could have used one yesterday)—and decided that might be the pie you make while you are waiting for the Island Time Pie to bake.

Note: Sue Ten, dear, forgot to tell you that the Gay Whores for Christ Anonymous called to reserve The Swing Barn for their annual meeting on the 15th. I hope that's not the same night as the USCG Academy reunion. I know you can handle any possible conflict.

In other news, I wondered what we should have brought along with us for giveaways. I'm reminded of going on board the Russian trawler *Riga* some years ago, and wishing I had brought along a supply of ping pong balls to replace the ones they had lost as sea. Here, I wish I had brought Chiclets, bananas (lost to the island during the recent hurricane), and fishnet stockings, which are very popular among the female customs agents.

Outside of that, all I can say is that I do love a city where you can get beer out of vending machines. And if I were a drinking person, I might consider installing one in The Slice of Heaven 24-Hour Pie Shop and Driving Range.

We really did not spend four days in the Nassau Airport, it just felt that way. I also wished I'd brought along my clubs and some pink plastic practice balls. Oh yes. Those long empty halls just called for a little extra excitement.

Today's song is *Una Paloma Blanca*. If you can find a link, please post it. The little band at the roof top restaurant last night tried to play it for me, but they didn't actually know it so they played "Happy Birthday," some wonderful Beatles song which the mojitos have erased, and some other paloma song.

I was worried about not being able to go to sleep without reading—not to mention the far-from-normal consumption of caffeine & sugar of late—but I was able to swipe an English paperback from another fancier hotel's "library," plus I watched *The Motorcycle Diaries* in Spanish, which was just ideal.

Today we head out on a double-decker bus and pray for luggage. We miss you all.

What Do You Do?

One of the great pleasures of my recent trip with Little Peach to the land south of Key West was meeting The Philosopher Detective, traveling on his own while his dear partner Maggie was off for a reunion with some long-time chums.

We went through the usual tour-bus chat, which was laced with those wonderfully dry remarks that some people, perhaps, just don't get. For example, when I said I was an American, he said, "Someone has to be. Might as well be you." Yes, a philosopher.

Little Peach and I hit it off with him quite well, and the conversation flowed, in part—I think—because I no longer have to explain the incomprehensible nature of my former employment.

I did have a brief visit down that road, but The Philosopher Detective quickly pointed out my mistake by saying, "Quite a conversation stopper, that one."

Yes, indeed. It is such a delight these days to be able to say to people, who care to ask 'What do you do?" that I own a pie shop. And a driving range. I tell you, there are damn few people who don't like one or the other.

You should have seen how the little Cuban boys reacted when I told them that I own a pie shop!

Tale of a Pink Hat

The first pink hat was actually a pair, from a time long ago, when the kids were eleven, and we were doing the grand tour of our nation's capitol, staying at a friend's house in Annapolis, and riding in on the train. Somewhere along the line, I had acquired two bright pink hats with the Pink Panther on them.

I think they came free with insulation, and at that time in life, we were very well insulated. Now remember, this was in the days before cell phones and just slightly after the days in which we all felt pretty safe letting our kids run around with minimal supervision.

We did great with the hats, and I could spot the twins tearing around from a pretty good distance. We did great, that is, until we arrived at the National Zoo shortly before a bus load of school kids arrived, all wearing, you know it, hot pink hats. Hundreds of them.

Fortunately, my two skinny children and I did still find each other at the appointed spot and the appointed time, but since that trip, a pink hat reminds me of a special time in my life when "family" was the three of us with our over-sized glasses and over-sized vocabularies, and we were quite happy to explore just about anything together.

The next pink hat is one that I never actually owned, an opportunity lost when The Morning Guy one day went off to a ball game & left me a note saying to call if I wanted him to pick up anything. I couldn't think of a thing. "Like what?" I scrawled on the note. Imagine my surprise when I later saw his immaculate tiny printing that said, "I thought you might have liked one of those pink hats."

I was stunned. I hadn't worn any kind of ball cap for years, just wide-brimmed girlie hats like Rene Russo in the movie *Tin Cup*, but had come to like the idea of a pink hat, free of team color and all that, but still definitely a treasure. I especially loved seeing more and more pink hats showing up at Spring Training, no matter what teams might be on the field. I did, in fact, want one of those hats.

Of course, you and I both know that was a one-time only offer. He will not make a similar suggestion again. He will, likely, make some other offer, and I will probably be obtuse enough to miss that one, too.

In my mind, the pink ball cap would fit me perfectly, covering my ears just so, but there's still the nagging doubt that it might have had the wrong team logo on it. I've been tempted, as you can imagine, to buy my own pink hat, possibly a Red Sox one, but even that will not fill the void of the gift not accepted. I can easily obtain the hat. It's the gifting that I want.

Now, I could ramble on here about gifting for quite a long time, but I know you have other things to do, so let's just move up to the present day, and even more hats. I like to go to Miami once a year and meet up with some of my former colleagues to find out how they are doing.

This year, I was delighted when some of the folks from New Zealand brought along some ball caps with their company logo on them. I was even more delighted when my Dutch friends said they could do better than that, and quickly produced a pink hat. Perfect, or almost perfect. A gift. Pink. I could add the Red Sox logo to it later.

This was all shortly before Little Peach and I headed south, lost our luggage, and began to tour The Island for four days in the same clothes. I wore white slacks, which grew less and less white, a yellow sleeveless golf shirt (which I eventually supplemented with a Cuban tee-shirt), walking shoes, and my pink hat.

As I've mentioned before, I wished I had known what to take to give away or trade with people, and now I really know: Chiclets, fishnet hose, pads of paper, and pink hats. I would outfit the entire population of Havana with pink hats. But I would have to do it in a roundabout way. The gnarly old man who first took a liking to my hat was not, as it turned out, all that interested in the hat, but what he might get for it.

Is this how capitalism takes over? I don't know. I had already given him more than enough in coin for a week old newspaper, but the hat was what kept him standing in front of me, smiling. I understood. I took it off and handed it over. He smiled some more. He kissed the hat. He walked away with it, and Little Peach and I watched him go. In fact, we continued to watch him from the tour bus, and we saw the next exchange take place, as the pink hat moved right along for a few coins.

And then we watched as the vendor who bought it examined it, checked it all out, and examined it again. As he did that, a new customer appeared and made an offer. It must have been a good one, since before we knew it, the hat was being slipped into a bag and the transaction was complete.

I'm curious about the bag, though. That means whoever bought it did not plan to wear it. Perhaps a gift, perhaps one that was absolutely perfect.

Full Moon, Clouds, and Wind (Part Two)

We had a problem with the lights last night. They strobed for a bit, then went out completely just as the full moon (now waning gibbous) rose above the clouds. At about the same time, the wind came up not gusting but steady, and I will admit the combination was sheer energy.

We brought out a few emergency lamps for those who wanted them. For the rest of us, it was an excellent exercise in ninja hurricane full-moon golf, looking not at the ball but just to the left and path it would take if only we could see that far.

Sparkle Junior brought out the E-Z Cart and turned on the headlights to give us a little more illumination, but after a few shots, we all said turn the damn lights off. We listened to the whacks and the misses, muttered our mantras, and continued with the dance for a good half hour in the moonlight before artificial power kicked in and took over once again.

I'm thinking today about vision and motion, and how hard it is not to look at the ball, even when I know I'll have a better hit if I find a drizdi point to hold my vision. My body still hasn't learned to trust the swing, but it will get there.

The last night in Havana, Little Peach crashed early, and I went out into the Cuban night on my own, ended up dancing with strangers for hours, and my body remembered the dance steps just like I knew it would.

It was a couple of days later when it dawned on me that only one of my new friends actually spoke English, and yet the conversation was eloquent in so many ways.

Sometimes, it seems, words are my enemy. Or at least not my best friend. Sometimes, it seems, I learn so much more by dancing all night or by hitting golf balls into the dark, into the wind.

The point here is this: I can trust my body to remember dance steps and yoga poses; therefore, it is only a matter of time before the elusive consistent swing becomes part of the package, and I do look forward to that.

Today's golf tip: Believe.

The Best Photos are the Ones I Never Took

I had an interesting talk with Little Peach about this concept, and how I feel that some pictures cannot be captured by a camera, but are better left in one's mind. She disagreed, and said she felt she could have and would have taken the shots. I don't know.

I think the camera can be too much of a wall, and I'd rather have the closeness of your magic rubbing up against mine, no molecules in between. Here are three that I did not take:

Just a glimpse into an apartment as we walk from the Malacon back to Marti Square. The lighting is dim, like in one of Paul Strand's WPA photos of Appalachia or the Dust Bowl. The living room is illuminated only by an old television, and an even older man sits in dark pants and bright white tee-shirt, watching some show in Spanish with a little boy on his lap, ignoring the press of people walking by.

Stopping by the corner of a church, I want to be blessed by a huge black woman, all in white lace, smoking a monstrous cigar. I have no time for a full reading of her cards so I just give her my coin and ask to be blessed. She does as I ask and laughs, slipping that cigar back into her pink toothless mouth. I can still see the red backs of the cards laid out among all that white. I can still smell the spritz of lavender on my hair and hands.

Little Peach and I are riding on the top of the "hop on, hop off bus," sipping our beers. She is letting her hair fly back as we cruise the roadway across from the Morro Castle. She's singing a little "Soul sister, go sister," but she doesn't know the words. I sing them for her: "Voulez-vous couchez avec moi, ce soir," and she confesses she does not know what they mean, which makes me laugh with delight. "Hey, Joe, you want to give it a go?" And then we both sing, raising our bottles of Bucanero beer on our way down the Malacon at night.

But You Look So Cuban

As you might imagine, I'm still trying to hold on to my memories of Cuba before they flit away, but it's been difficult finding the time to write to all-you-all, what with so much to do just now at The Pie Shop and Driving Range.

I didn't sleep well last night, but you already know how that waning gibbous moon affects me, and I've had some strange dreams lately about The Morning Guy. In one of these dreams, he and I are in some kind of Main Street U.S.A. Theme Park in a huge crowd, which is always trouble for me.

I had no information about what was going on, but he was carrying something the size of the menu at Denny's or IHOP, and kept asking me if I wanted to sign up for any of the special activities, and he had already marked the ones that he thought I should do.

I don't remember the other dream half as well, but again there was a crowd, and confusion beyond anything that I ever see anywhere near my turquoise conch cottage. And again The Morning Guy was with me, close enough to touch, guiding me to wherever it was we needed to go. How he knew the route, I cannot say. After all, it was a dream.

Still, Sparkle Junior is pretty well convinced now that The Morning Guy was, at sometime in his past, a secret agent. Personally, I still think he's Canadian.

There's so much we don't know about him, but he does know how to hit a golf ball, and he does savor a nice piece of pie, and that's all we need to know right now. I wish I could have brought him back a cigar or two.

He's a blessing to us, especially now that the snow birds are arriving. So many of them require an extra bit of attention, both in the shop and out on the range, and I deal with them so much better when I have my Post-Its and emails from The Morning Guy to keep me on task.

A few years ago, I wrote a series of essays that I called "Unwelcome Blessings" and perhaps you remember some of those stories. If not, let me know, and I'll send you a copy. In Cuba, I welcomed blessings, and received many.

I've already told you about paying a peso to be blessed by the Santeria woman, but there were others.

For one, it was a blessing to spend so much time with Little Peach, that goes without saying. I also found a blessing in wandering out by myself, into a circle of people on Marti square. As it turns out, they were young Christians, close to rapture, and I was glad to let them surround me with their prayers.

And I was just as glad to walk away and open another can of Bucanero beer as soon as I was out of sight. Of course, the moment that I did that, their pastor appeared next to me, and gave me a smile. I'm sure that was a blessing, too, since we'd already had a lovely chat about Jesus and the miracle of the wine.

I also found a blessing in the words, "But you look so Cuban."

I heard that in three different situations, and on each occasion I felt a glow in my heart, as well as a bit of mystification in my mind, especially the last time when the speaker was so obviously European and was hoping I had some local knowledge to impart.

I did not. My understanding of Havana is fragile and untested. I suspect it will not last for long.

So, today I'm sorting out my memories and trying to recall the rest of my dream about The Morning Guy. As I do this, I'm remembering that these activities call on different parts of my mind.

I used to give my writing students a three-part assignment: Describe someone from memory, from observation, and from imagination.

What I didn't understand then is what would happen to my written observations, my notes. Those seemingly hard facts have blended now into fantasy, and maybe I have already waited too long to tell you my story. But maybe alchemy will take over and turn my thoughts into a metal that you can cast.

Chocolate Cuban-Rum Pie

Ingredients

    3/4 cup Caribbean sugar

    pinch salt

    1 C milk

    1 envelope unflavored gelatin

    2 eggs, separated

    6 oz dark, rich chocolate

    1/3 C Santiago rum.

> *Note: Don't waste your time with Havana Club or Bacardi. (Some travel and an undisguised willingness to smuggle home the good stuff may be required.)*

    1 C whipping cream

    1 t vanilla extract

    1 shortbread-crumb pie shell, ready to go

Directions

1. Combine 1/2 C of the sugar, salt, and milk (reserving 2 T for later).

2. In a small bowl, mix the remaining milk with the unflavored gelatin.

3. In yet another small bowl, beat the egg yolks until fluffy beyond your wildest dreams.

4. Heat and stir the milk and sugar until the sugar is dissolved.

> *Remember to let this cool to a pleasant and somewhat tropical room temperature, and then*

blend in the eggs. (If the milk is too hot, you'll poach the eggs. Take care.)

5. Stir and stir and stir. Heat the mixture until it thickens, and quickly—and with style and grace—add the gelatin and the wonderful dark pieces of chocolate.

6. Now for the best part: Chill. You know what I mean.

7. When the mixture is just starting to set, add the rum.

8. Chill for a bit longer. Stir and chill. Chill and stir. Don't let time be a factor. Go by your sense of taste and texture.

9. Beat the egg whites until they form soft peaks, then add the rest of the sugar.

10. Fold the egg whites into the rum-laced chocolate.

11. Whip up the cream and add the vanilla.

12. Whisper a blessing into your pie shell and patiently layer the chocolate and the cream, one after another.

13. Give it all one decisive swirl with your favorite spatula.

14. Think of me dancing in the Havana night, and enjoy your pie.

My Map of Havana

Not easily read,
the compass rose pointing
to directions unknown
where I want to travel
with or without caffeine and chocolate
with or without your side-snaking dance steps
with or without your purple sedan.

I already know
the taste of mojito
on my tongue before morning.

I already know
how to sing in a language
that does not need words.

I already know
the alleyway music
that goes on without me
and maps a new route
that plays through my hands.

I wish you had been there.

I wish you had seen
the architects' angels
that cast shadows
around me
and drew their own maps
on my brow and my soul.

As I look at my map now
the street music swelters
and fades into the fumes
and Ladas and Fiats
while tourists and families
ride on the bus tops,
drive homemade bike rickshaws,
line up at the bakeries,
and dive from the rocks
into the water
that protects and divides them,
gives shape to the map.

Karaoke Golf

It's Friday night, and my sister Melbie is here and she wants to sing karaoke at The Swing Barn with some of the other gals. Normally, I don't care that much for karaoke, but Sue Ten's wide screen really is big enough for me to see the words, so I'm thinking I should join Mel when I am done with my practice.

For some reason, there are more little girls on the range than I have ever seen before. I am making a mental note to myself to have The Morning Guy check into ordering some of those wicked cute little pink golf sets so we can capitalize on this trend.

At the same time, I'm a little disheartened to see nine-year olds in pink shorts and wild, curly, uncombable hair driving balls almost twice as far as I can. Yet.

As I listen and watch, I understand what The Morning Guy meant when he told me that some golf tips, notably Tip Number 2 and Tip Number 3, must be demonstrated. I hope some day he will get around to doing that for me.

I watch a dad with one of the little girls as he demonstrates again and again the rhythm that he wants her to mimic. She listens, she hits, and her drive is good. Then the dad says, "Now do that again three more times," and she bursts into tears.

Granted, this is after almost an hour of relentless coaching, but it breaks my heart. Her two younger sisters ignore the entire scene, and soon I see all three of the little girls following Sparkle Junior around as he picks up empty ball buckets and takes them back to the shop.

The dad meanwhile hits a dozen or so balls before collecting his cool and gathering up his girls to go inside for some peppermint ice cream pie with an oreo-cookie crust. He wins me over once again.

My own practice seems odd since I am watching the clock, and that's not something I normally do anymore. Typically, I take all the time I want to hit 100 or more balls: No one is waiting on me, no one is looking for me, no one is calling my name, and I love that freedom.

I find it odd to be rushing to meet Melbie, but I am compulsive about being on time, and the rushing, in fact, does not seem to have any great affect on my results. What I'm missing, I think, is not so much improvement in my game, but the leisure to enjoy the details.

I'll also tell you that I'm looking forward to hearing Melbie sing. I know she'll outshine everyone there, and will totally surprise the folks who don't already know her. Sue Ten and I will warm them up with "Benny and the Jets," but Melbie will knock them out with "Desperado."

I'm remembering riding through Havana on the bus top with Little Peach, who wanted me to sing some blues for her. I had offered jug-band, but she said no no no. She grew up with jug-band music and could not longer abide it. I start to sing "I Can't Make You Love Me," and she stops me on that, too. "I want blues, but not sad," she says. And I am stumped.

As I finish up my last few hits, I know the song I should have sung, and I hope it's on Sue Ten's karaoke machine: "Double-Bogey Blues." It's a good night, and I am ready to sing. I hope you are, too, but remember what I always say: "Introverts with microphones: A dangerous combination."

Fried Steak in Space

I remember the first argument that I ever had with my second ex-husband Pretty Boy Boyd. When I told the twins about it, Chandler said, "You mean you finally told him that you really don't like Irish music?"

"No," I replied. "I told him that I fry steak."

Pretty Boy had almost walked out of my life right then and there, but sadly, he changed his mind, and spent the next several years trying to convince me that the hours it takes to perfectly BBQ a steak Kansas-City style somehow produce a finer meal than the five minutes it takes to drop a fine piece of beef into a super-hot salted skillet and cook it cowboy style.

This past week, a British fragrance firm—Omega Ingredients—reported that it had been contracted by NASA to identify the aroma of space. The results are in, my dear friends, and sure enough space smells like fried steak. (Note: I am not entirely convinced that this news is not a spoof.)

I immediately went to the NASA website to investigate further, but when I typed "fried steak" into the search box, all that came up was the week's NASA Exchange Cafeteria menu, which sure enough did include a $5.00 Fried Steak Dinner for the week of October 20 to 24.

I know I cannot offer that value for your dollar at Slice of Heaven 24-Hour Pie Shop and Driving Range, but maybe I can offer you a slice of fried-steak pie for supper, but only if you put your order in early. I don't want to miss the Red Sox on the big screen at The Swing Barn tonight.

But I digress.

As I tried to find the official NASA word on steak in space, I came across a reference to an interesting short story by Terry Bisson titled, "They're Made Out of Meat." While some say the odor of space is "a high energy vibration in the molecule," others says Bisson's story and screenplay both more fully explain the space-steak aroma phenomenon.

The Things That They Took

The bookshelves in The Pie Shop are still looking a little sparse, so I'm adding a few volumes to them today, starting with anything written by Martin Cruz Smith. Everywhere in Cuba, especially when we were near the Malecon, I saw scenes out of *Havana Bay* with Russian investigator Arkady Renko continuing his tortured comprehension of good and evil. Arkady would never be one to say, "It's all good." I always liked that about him.

I'm also going to donate my copy of *Slim and None* by Dan Jenkins, mostly for his character Grady Don whose flatstick had health problems, starting with diabetes-meningitis and going on to include heart trouble, flu, ulcers, and constipation. He had one that spoke to him—not in a civil tone—and one that could swim.

Grady Don said, "The best thing you can do with a putter that betrays you is kill the sumbitch," but there's more. "Make sure it's dead." That one that could swim? It grew fins and worked the beaches waiting for a chance to bite the leg off a vacationing golfer.

In the end, Grady Don concluded that "nobody could manufacture a putter that wouldn't catch syphilis eventually." You've been warned.

My golf instructor Sandra recently gave me a putter, and I bought another one at Goodwill. In either case, I need to have one or the other re-gripped, which is not a problem since my sister Melbie gave me a gift certificate at the "Putter Around" golf shop for just such a project. The question I have now is, "Why bother? It's just going to betray me or die an untimely death anyway."

Another book that I am adding to The Pie Shop shelves is *The Things That They Carried* by Tim O'Brien. What I've always loved about that book is the chapter listing quite precisely what they—a platoon of soldiers in Vietnam—carried in their packs.

O'Brien created a litany from what might have been a mundane list, and now college freshmen everywhere are challenged to figure out how he did it.

Having finally retrieved my errant luggage from BahamasAir, I find myself creating my own catalog, no where as poignant as O'Brien's, but a tribute nonetheless as I mull over "the things that they took."

I can't claim to know who "they" might be in this case, and I've already written about tossing my pink hat into the stream of commerce in Havana. That was choice. Inventorying the items missing from my luggage has been another exercise altogether, a last chance to remember some articles that I will never see again, and never replace.

So, what were the things that they took?

They took all the jewelry out of a ziplock bag, one I'd tossed into my so-called carry-on as an afterthought. They left they bag but took the necklaces, four that I can recall: a hand-carved dolphin that my former boss Chris gave me before I left Maine for my ill-fated move to Missouri, a silver square cross from Argentina, a blue glass pendant from last summer's trip to Burano, and a bit of Roman glass that I bought on our cruiseship.

They took my fake gold Chinese Rolex, one of three that I brought back from Zhuhai. Can you believe it still worked?

They took two sterling rings, each depicting a dragon of sorts, one Celtic, one more abstract. My dragon rings served to remind me of the protective dragons that had started to visit me in meditations during a bad time, years ago. I still have those imaginary dragons, I don't really need the rings anymore.

I'll miss the bracelets they took, one made of Venetian glass beads and another that was a cheap "wishing bracelet," a twin of one I'd given Little Peach when taking a cruise in Europe was on our minds but not yet in our reality. Now it's a memory.

They took a copy of *World War Z*, a birthday gift from a surprising colleague. A year ago, he gave me a gift for the first time, a copy of William Gibson's *Pattern Recognition*, saying "I hope you haven't read this."

I had read it, in tandem with *The Tipping Point*, and I thoroughly enjoyed reading it a second time, following up with two more Gibson books during the next few months. I didn't even get to browse *World War Z*, but I'll buy a new copy and read it soon. It won't be the same.

They took the birthday card that was with the book. They left the envelope.

They took my new prescription sunglasses. I suspect they'll have to knock out the lenses for them to be of any use, my eyesight is so peculiar. They also took a pair of red-framed computer glasses, the ones that I am wearing in my Beast Empress portrait by James Harvey as part of his "100 Pirates in 100 Days Project."

They left the oversized glasses case, and inside I found a fortune that I'd gotten from a cookie a few weeks ago: "A big fortune will descend upon you this year." I just can't remember where I got the cookie.

They took a black bra, the first one I bought after losing weight and discovering I'd been wearing the wrong size, too big in girth, too small in mass.

They took my orange bra, an impulse buy at Victoria's Secret, expensive and satisfying, one I'd worn on every trip, short or long, since May. And they took the straps to a beige convertible bra, but left the bra itself, which shall now be forever strapless.

They took a folder of papers, bills, and other documents that I fully intended to address on vacation. At least, I think that's what became of them.

They took my blue New Zealand hat, the one that inspired the gift of the pink hat.

And lastly, they took my little six-dollar alarm clock from Walgreen's. I suspect that they were after the batteries. Now when I wake up in the night, I have to look at my call phone to see what time it is. I can't tell you how wrong that is. I liked that clock since it didn't glow or warble or tick. It just was. And now it is. Somewhere else.

Perhaps, I shall have to call on the allegiance of the Beast Empress's legions and go get it all back. Perhaps not.

Museums: Pie and Revolution

I've been wondering about adding a Pie Museum to The Slice of Heaven 24-Hour Pie Shop and Driving Range. It seems to me that it might draw in a few more people in the off season, and besides that I like the idea. There's certainly no shortage of golf museums and golf halls of fame, but pie appears to have been short shrifted.

I'm sure that there are some glorious pie paintings, prints, and drawings that I could install there. I already know of several sculptures, or at least ceramics. Several movies have certainly featured pie: whipped cream pie, shaving cream pie, warm apple pie, and other varieties. I always liked the John Travolta movie *Michael*, in which he played an angel, supposedly the very one who invented pie, and it includes a lovely scene of Andie McDowell singing about pie. Then there's the more recent movie *Waitress*, and on network television, there's *Pushing Daisies* about a piemaker with the touch of life, or death.

Perhaps I can also include some history of pie, science of pie, and the future of pie. There's a lot of pie memorabilia, not to mention equipment, costuming, and cookery. For example, there's that four-and-twenty blackbirds story. Perhaps you'd like to know more about that. Let me know. The museum is just in the planning stages, and we have plenty of time to get it right. Perhaps we can come up with something as appealing as Cranberry World in Plymouth, Massachusetts, or even the World's Largest Teflon Frying Pan.

I like all kinds of museums, ranging from the tiny one that used to be—and maybe still is—in Silver Plume,

Colorado, back in the days when local residents freely grew pot plants in the window-boxes of their homes, to the utterly fantastic Provincial Museum in British Columbia.

My favorite fictional museum is the Barnum Museum in the book by the same name, written by Stephen Millhauser who also wrote the short story that became the movie *The Illusionist*.

In Havana, though, my favorite place in the city was the Museum of the Revolution.

When I sent my dear friend Ms. Jay my a copy of the collage I made from Cuban currency and receipts, she wrote back that she was very glad that I had been to the Museum of the Revolution, and said, "I could picture you looking at the wax sculptures of Che and Camilo coming out of the jungle."

Yes, and I could see her there, too. For me, the Museum was the high point of the trip, my primary reason for being there on the island South of Key West.

The building itself was once the dictator Batista's palace, and the ornate architecture said a lot about that time and place when there was such a huge gap between the haves and the have-nots. Revolution, indeed.

Our tour guide Michel Ten told us a story about a group of students who tried to storm the palace in Batista's days, but Batista easily escaped through one of the many secret tunnels. The students? They did not survive their act of revolution.

What drives a people to revolution? Extremes, and that was very clear just in seeing the contrast of the building, and imagining it as it once had been, with the simple displays, and open windows, and peeling paint on the interior walls.

I'm sure the displays in the Museum of the Revolution did not meet the standards of even the most

The Slice of Heaven

basic interpretation in the Smithsonian, and yet I don't remember ever being so moved by a museum, so touched. I once read an essay in which a young boy visiting the British Museum reported back that the thing he loved best was Lord Nelson's shirt, "with his own blood on it."

Everything in the Museum of the Revolution, it seemed, had someone's own blood on it. And, yes, that's what I like best, too. Nothing really cleaned up or laundered. Nothing polished or restored. But room after room, in what had once been a fabulous palace, I read and saw the tale of an island and its people, their struggles, and their blood.

The lack of artifacts was what spoke to me the loudest: a placard related the story of a hero, and then in the case, a piece of cutlery with a note: "Here is a spoon he once used." For another, a pair of cuff-links. Letters from Fidel, written in perfect Palmer-method penmanship. Photographs of friends and comrades, in good times and bad.

I read recently, that people who grew up in the time of black and white television are more prone to dream in black and white, rather than in color. I dream in color.

And I don't know where that quite fits in here, except to remind me to tell you that nearly all the photos in this museum were black and white, and as we went through the rooms, we eventually came to one with a black and white television—an *old* black and white television—playing a continuous loop showing a plane landing, and then two soldiers solemnly coming down the stairs, with the box containing Che's remains hoisted on their shoulders.

Not a coffin. A box. No pretense that all of Ernesto Che Guevara's remains were there, so much gone already into the earth or scattered.

I sat in my gray-metal folding chair in the unbearable brightness of the room and watched the loop again and again, until I felt I could finally move on to the next section where, indeed, I did see the wax figures of Che and Camilo, running out of the jungle.

A crowd of school children had come into the museum earlier, surging around me as I squatted to read the inscriptions next to weapons and cufflinks. By then, I'd been asked a couple of times by adults if I were Cuban, but the kids had no doubt that I was a foreigner in their midst. They looked at me with curiosity, but also with comradeship, explained things to me in slow careful Spanish, which I did not understand as much as I felt—very deeply—the effort they were taking to talk to me, and then they ran ahead to point at their next favorite item or display.

By the time I caught up with them again, two of the boys, maybe nine or ten years old, were posing in front of the wax figures of Che and Camilo, running out of the jungle; two young boys, eerily wearing the same solemn faces as the soldiers who had carried the remains down the stairs from the plane. No joking, no fooling around.

Even now, my mind is full of those images of artifacts in tattered cases, and unsmiling school boys who have learned well the message of work, learn, and fight.

But then, all I could do was to wipe my eyes, find Little Peach at the edge of the crowd, and walk down the sweeping Scarlett O'Hara staircase to the floor below.

We next went into the ballroom, filled with gilt-edged mirrors which, I'm sure, only hinted at how opulent the building had really once been. Our eyes were drawn up to the grandiose mural on the ceiling, and I lay down on the floor to see the whole thing.

As I did, coins clattered out of my white-pants pockets all around me, echoing hollowly through the room. I gathered them up and lay down again, Little Peach guiding me to the best spot to see the host of angels and also the fire that they were dousing. A crystal chandelier hung down from the center of that ferocious heaven, and I lay on my back below, looking up and thinking of Che and Camilo running out of the jungle, and the unsmiling boys.

No one told me not to lie on the floor. Then again, no one else joined me there.

I felt colorless and pale as we left the building and headed back up the street toward the Museum of Contemporary art, a modern structure built around an open courtyard and sculpture garden.

We started at the top and began to work our way down, but I did not find much there that appealed to me, so I left Little Peach on her careful and thoughtful stroll and went down to the courtyard to reflect on what I'd seen—perfect, temperature-controlled and well-lighted painting and sculpture—and I wondered at the sadness that pervaded everything for me.

Perhaps the sorrow was left over from the Museum of the Revolution, or maybe it was a sense of art that was never allowed to blossom fully, kept in check somehow. The impressionist paintings there all reminded me of the French masters, but they seemed to be copies, not originals. And the more recent images seemed to be pervaded with death, disease, famine, and pestilence.

I wanted more originality, more spirit. I wanted the Cuban art of the murals and the streets to find its way into the fine galleries of the world, too. The art museum left me feeling unsettled and unhappy. Drowsy, I rested on a bench and watched a busload of teenagers in red tee-shirts milling around outside the museum doors.

In time, Little Peach joined me, lifting my spirits, and we sauntered companionably back up the street to our hotel, at an easy pace, not at all like Che and Camilo running out of the jungle.

Pumpkin Cheesecake Pie

A few weeks ago, some of the girls and I got together for what I thought was to be an "Evening in India," but it turned out to be a continuation of my month-long birthday celebration. What a treat! We had a lovely time sitting by the pool over at Pancho Villas, the new Over-55 gated community, and then we had quite a bit of Indian food for dinner, punctuated with photo ops, and followed by a screening of the Bollywood movie *Water*.

The only thing missing, we decided, was pumpkin cheesecake. I should mention here that we did have pumpkin pie, and we did have cheesecake, too, and while alternating bites was certainly delicious, the combo would have been even better, so I promised to add a pumpkin-cheesecake pie recipe to The Slice of Heaven menu, and here it is.

For the crust

Make a graham-cracker crust. Surely you know how to do that by now. Cinnamon grahams are the best for this spicy sort of concoction.

For the filling

1 1/2 C canned pumpkin
3 eggs, the larger the better
1 1/2 t cinnamon
1/2 t nutmeg
1 t ginger
1/2 t salt
1/2 C dark brown sugar—pack it in there
24 oz softened cream cheese
1/2 C sugar

2 T whipping cream
1T cornstarch
1 t pure vanilla
Dash of bourbon
For the topping
2 C sour cream
2 T sugar

Another dash of bourbon, maybe a little more generous now.

Preparation

Make the crust and chill. *Don't skimp on the "chill" part.*

Whisk together the pumpkin, eggs, spices, salt, and brown sugar.

Cream the cream cheese and sugar, then whip in the cream, cornstarch, vanilla, and booze.

Add the pumpkin mix, and keep at it until it's all smooth and mellow.

Get out your chilled crust and fill it up with this lovely mixture.

Bake in the middle of the oven at 350°F for 50 to 55 minutes.

Test for doneness with a toothpick, Then place the pie on a rack to cool.

Meanwhile, whisk together the sour cream, sugar, and bourbon..

Spread the topping over the pie and bake it for another five minutes, and you are good to go.

The Philosopher Detective

Little Peach stopped in at The Pie Shop the other day to show me some of the photos she took on our trip to Havana, and to reminisce a bit, especially about our dinner with The Philosopher Detective.

I wish we had a good photo of him to show you. I know you probably think we made him up, but really he was our companion for an afternoon and evening, and quite a remarkable one at that.

We met him on our bi-lingual bus tour, the one during which I gave away my pink hat, as you may recall. By the way, I did look at a possible pink-hat replacement when I was in Costa Rica, but it still was not the same; nor was the one that I found today at the local thrift shop with "Vail" embroidered on it. Perhaps next spring I'll buy a Red Sox one after all.

To continue, as we all toured the Morro Castle, The Philosopher Detective and I began to chat, and then we compared our purchases back on the bus. He'd bought rum and cigars for friends, and I'd bought a single dark-rum nip for myself. Until that point, he may well have been one of the people who thought I was a Cuban. (In my memory now, as you can imagine, most people did.)

I told him I'd only bought the nip to drink on the bus since I couldn't take any of the lovely stuff home. "I'm an American," I said and, as you recall, he won me over when he replied, "I suppose someone has to be. Might as well be you."

By the time we reached the walking tour part of our program, Little Peach knew much of his life history, including his long relationship with the marvelous Maggie, who was off on her own holiday with friends from way back when. By the time we all three decided to drop the tour and go off by ourselves for dinner, we were fast friends, at least for the one evening.

First, though, our tour guide led us into an establishment undoubtedly run by friends of his. We caught on to that when we noticed that the bartender already had an icy mojito waiting for him the minute that we walked in the door. The place—a faux Irish pub complete with regulation mariachi band—was touted as yet another Hemingway waterhole. I think it's safe to say that there was no drinking establishment in Havana where Hemingway did not knock back a pop or two.

We settled in upstairs, where we were pretty much a captive audience, for "a break," and shelled out a bit of cash for mojitos and beer, applauding on cue for the band. I could see that both The Philosopher Detective and Little Peach were getting a little antsy, but I wasn't sure why until we were out on the pavement again, and TPD burst out saying, "It was all I could do to keep from leaping over the table to free that poor bird from its cage."

Yes, a man of passion, and that's when he won Little Peach, too. Allow me to insert a little background note here: If you were to arrive at Little Peach's house with your car windshield smashed and cracked beyond belief, and perhaps even a shard or two of glass wedged into your forehead, she would help you mop up the blood, but she would first want you to go back and check on the health of the bird that you'd hit. (Yes, that's one of the many reason we love her, isn't it?)

TPD was cut of the same cloth, and we were delighted to discover that he knew of a charming rooftop restaurant where we would continue our conversation at leisure. The lower level of the place was a jazz bar, and the music was dead-on perfect. We passed by the mahogany bar and beckoning chairs and entered the tiny grill-worked elevator that took us to the roof, where we were treated to a view of Morro Castle, the harbor, and the sea at dusk.

To our surprise, our waiter was reluctant to offer recommendations for dinner, but he explained that it was his first day on the job and he could not yet personally vouch for the quality of the food. I thought that was an interesting perspective, rather than telling us, "It's all good."

Once we had ordered at our own risk, TPD told us about his career in London, conducting investigations and interrogations, and we learned that the most valuable weapon in his considerable arsenal was silence. "Yes," he said, "more often than not, you'll find out what you want to know if you can just out-wait the poor fool you're questioning."

I've understood that myself, by intuition, but I've never been able to put it into practice. I always crack first and spit out another question. What about you? Let's try it sometime. We also talked about humor and writing and learning to live a new life.

I've done that as you know, and so has TPD, when his career as a working detective suddenly ended as his body collapsed and he found himself in a hospital bed, rather than at the scene of the next crime. His dark world, in which he well knew the difference between the living, the just-dead, and the long-dead, rapidly shifted into one in which he knew he had to find a better way to live, and to communicate.

An introspective man, he shared his regrets and joys, with an self-questioning aspect that we enjoyed tremendously, as he played both the interrogator and subject in his own story. Part of the tale included a period in which he gained so much weight that he had become whale-like in proportion, but then took extreme measures to drop back down to "normal" size. "What a pleasure it is," he said, "just to go into a shop and buy clothes ready made. What a joy, just to walk down the street next to my Maggie, not lagging behind so people would not know I was with her."

"I wondered about that," I surprised myself by saying, "because you walk like a fat man, but you really are not fat at all." Yes, he did have that slow deliberate step, as if the ground might crumble beneath him, and he knew it. I know what it is like to lose 35 pounds, but he'd lost 140!

As the evening danced on, we listened to the rooftop band play traditional Cuban music, heard the canon at the Castle fire, watched the sunlight fade, and saw the full moon rise among the dark tumbling clouds. We talked of families, lovers, friends, travel, books, *The Wind in the Willows*, and everything else that touched our hearts at that particular moment in time, and we topped it off with some ice cream that the waiter could not identify.

"It's tiramisu," I told him, after a taste or two or three. TPD and Little Peach nodded in agreement. Yes. Tiramisu ice cream for dessert, on a rooftop in Havana. Before we pushed back our chairs and headed to the elevator, I asked TPD how many people he thought were sitting behind him. The terrace restaurant had been pretty much empty when we arrived. "Six," he guessed. "Turn around," I said. There were 18 people seated at one long table, just getting up to fill their plates at a buffet.

When I see people come into The Pie Shop and become so engrossed in conversation that they don't even see the other people in the room, I'm always a bit jealous. Then again, I feel that pleasant isolation so often myself when you and I have the chance to talk the way that we do, connecting on so many levels. Let's do it again real soon.

Hollywood Halloween

I still need to scrape the glitter off my face after last night's Hollywood Halloween. Yes, I know that yesterday was really All Soul's Day, but we're talking Hollywood, and we had to take into account the writers' strike and other details that might conceivably caused a slight delay in our participation in festivities here at The Slice of Heaven 24-Hour Pie Shop and Driving Range. I'm pretty sure, too, that we weren't the only ones running a day late, or even a dollar short.

I'd thought that everyone would have been pretty much costumed out, especially after Sue Ten's usual high-tone event over at The Swing Barn on Friday night, but you know how it is once people get into too much sugar and dressing-up. They just want more, more, more.

The first arrivals walked in to The Pie Shop around 8:00 p.m., and we served up some of that nice Pumpkin Pie Cheesecake that the India Night girls are always craving. Just for fun, I wore a pink and white waitress costume, modeled on the one in the movie *Waitress*. I had also pulled on my blonde French-twist wig and applied the blue eyeshadow and glitter liberally. I wanted to chew gum, too, but I'm one of those people without the gum-chewing gene and it prevents me from doing anything else very well.

Joe Sparkle Junior dressed as The Morning Guy, which I thought was especially funny, and Sue Ten came in for a while in full geisha girl regalia.

She didn't stay for long, since it turned out she was really on her way to a dress rehearsal for a local production of *The Mikado*. She did drop off one of her wonderful pumpkin and potato casseroles seasoned with ginger and allspice, though. Delicious.

As always, we offered our "all the golf balls you can hit" rate of $10, but gave free balls to everyone who brought in some reasonably edible food to share, and before long, we had quite a line-up out on the range, under the lights which were unmercifully bright as we watched the sliver of a moon come up in the sky. People wandered in and out, balancing their paper plates full of chocolate brains, spicy guacamole dip, buffalo wings, organic celery, and watermelon Jell-o shots.

One of the girls came in a clown costume that was quite cheery and sweet at the beginning of the night, but grew increasingly frightening until by midnight the melting make-up made her look more and more like the Joker in the last Batman movie. Plus, after three or four margaritas that she'd smuggled over from The Swing Barn, she had developed the disconcerting habit of going up to people, just after they'd set up their shots, and she would leer at them and say, "Why so serious?" Then she'd launch into a chilling and maniacal laugh.

I had to ask her husband, Bob "He No Dead" Marley, to steer The Clown over to the picnic tables so people could work their drivers without a look of terror creeping over their faces. We soon discovered that feeding her chocolate-cinnamon mousse pie did nothing to calm her down, but deep-dish apple was a fairly reasonable antidote.

Earlier in the evening though, when The Clown was still pretty docile, I noticed that one of The Stepford Wives was blissfully welcoming her to the neighborhood and suggesting that she might want to join some of the other wives in their exercise and make-up classes.

"Really, my dear," said The Wife to The Clown, "you certainly do have a way with make-up and color, but you are in Stepford now, and you might want to tone down that look just a teeny little notch or two, and of course I am telling you this as a friend because I know we are going to be very, very good friends now, aren't we?"

The Clown continued to smile and nod, and The Wife continued to preach the virtues of living in Stepford, all the while smiling up at her handsome Stepford Husband as she repeatedly replaced the drink in his hand, the ball on his tee, and the cigarette in his mouth. Several of the regulars stood by and watched in amazement at this particular duo in their award-winning performance, which probably ended the minute they got into their SUV to drive home.

Another interesting couple was Joan Crawford and a Philadelphia Flyers hockey player. Joan was scolding him about using wire hangers, but he didn't seem to mind, and changed the topic to Philadelphia baseball, little knowing that Joan was a die-hard Red Sox fan.

"Once the Red Sox are out, who cares?" said Mommie Dearest.

"You're a Red Sox fan?" he asked suspiciously.

"Oh, yes," she said.

"I'm from New York," he said. "We are enemies."

Then he pivoted on his skates and stomped away. Thank god he was still in The Pie Shop and not out ruining my turf. Mommie Dearest just muttered "Spawn of Satan" and went on to wave her wire hanger at someone else.

Nearby, Wednesday from The Addams Family was giving some excellent golf tips to Nurse Mildred Ratched from *One Flew Over the Cuckoo's Nest*, but then Ratched was called away to administer medication to a tottering Amy Winehouse.

Neither Amy nor Ratched got in a single golf shot, but at least Amy didn't hurt anyone too badly when she fell down, again and again and again. By the end of her visit to the driving range, though, Nurse Ratched had transformed into Nurse Crotchett, and her performance had become increasingly X-rated. We all stopped to smoke a cigarette once she passed out beside Amy and lay quietly in the grass for the next hour or so.

Meanwhile, Mommie Dearest pointed out to me that the comatose Amy's bra strap had slipped own over her tattoo, and the strap was decidedly orange, not unlike the color of my formerly favorite bra, the one that did not return from the BahamasAir luggage system.

This prompted Wednesday Addams to give us a sweet little soliloquy about her days working at Victoria's Secret, and told us she had always been "the nice one" and never interrupted couples who were having sex in the changing rooms. Note to self: Always look for the most innocent clerk in sight when planning assignations at V.S., even in my mind.

I also noticed a number of James Bond lookalikes passing though, covering five decades of spy movies; one Terminator; two Incredible Hulks; numerous U.S. Presidents and presidential candidates; a dozen or so golfers ranging from The Shark to Spiderman to Happy Gilmore; Jason Varitek; several of The Baldwin Brothers, although they did not seem to know each other; and Joe the Plumber, who confessed that he was not even registered to vote.

Back in The Pie Shop, the cast of *Grease* took over the sound system and began singing "You're the one that I want ooh ooh ooh" until I pulled the plug on them and sent them over to The Swing Barn where the acoustics are better, or so I told them. Sue Ten will probably be calling me about that later on.

We did keep Sonny and Cher to ourselves, though, and set them up at a table where they could sign autographs and feed each other excessively gooey lemon-meringue pie. They were so cute, back in the early days. I'm sure you remember.

Around 10:00, we had a lull until a crew of Fem-Bot pirates arrived stark, raving sober, and in search of Georgia Peach Pie and coffee ice cream. When they'd had their fill of pie-booty and black coffee, they went out to the range and offered an astounding exhibition of synchronized golfing. Perhaps they were German pirates, I'm not sure. They were certainly efficient, and knew how to take the minimum amount of fabric to create the maximum amount of costume. Their ability to hit golf balls while wearing high-heeled boots was quite stunning, too.

This morning, as I said, we have a fair amount of clean-up to do, starting with my face. I may even break my no-caffeine rule and have a cup of Joe, the plain-Jane variety that I know you like so well. Remember, we do not serve lattes or mochachinos or frappacoffee or half-fat or low-fat or any other variation other than black or regular. You can put in your own sugar or Sweet N Low, and I really don't care how much or how little you use, as long as you remember to leave Sparkle a tip. He works hard at not spilling, and that should be rewarded. It's not as easy as it looks.

We hope you had a good weekend, too. Remember the time change, if you are somewhere where that happens. I'd forgotten, myself, but the clock in the kitchen has shifted, so I know The Morning Guy must have slipped in at some point in the night to make the fix. Now that I think of it, one of those James Bond boys did look strangely familiar.

Your Second-Cousin Darnell and the Goat

The other day, I saw a photo of a goat wearing sunglasses, and it reminded me of your second-cousin Darnell and his pet goat Jonathan.

It's not surprising that Darnell would have a goat as a pet, although I believe it was more of a business proposition at first.

Darnell seemed to think that the goat would be a zero-energy lawnmowing system for him, but he forgot about the residue that the goat would leave behind, not to mention the plain orneriness of goats in general. You can dress them up with big sunglasses, Hawaiian shirts, and hats, but down deep they are still goats.

We all got a good laugh out of it the first time that Darnell brought the goat by The Slice of Heaven 24-Hour Pie Shop and Driving Range, thinking I might want to pay for the Jonathan's lawn-chewing services, but I did not want the goat anywhere near my turf.

Sue Ten felt much the same way, although she did fall prey to the unfortunate idea that Jonathan could work as a bouncer for payday parties. Unfortunately, the goat did not exercise a lot of discretion about who to bounce and who to retain, so that idea was short-lived but memorable.

Jonathan pretty much stays home these days, in his little shed under the big ficus by Darnell's single-wide off Highway 441. I know Darnell would like to move to Pancho Villas closer to us, but they have a pretty well enforced no-goats rule, made all the stronger by the property manager who was one of the fools who picked up Darnell and Jonathan when they were hitchhiking to work at The Swing Barn.

Most reasonable people would not stop to pick up a man and a goat walking by the side of the road unless said reasonable people were driving a pick-up truck or maybe an animal-control van. At least, I hope they would not stop, especially once they saw that the man in question was indeed your second-cousin Darnell.

I think you were away when this happened, so you may not know why so many people now will not pick up Darnell under any circumstances.

Typically, the scenario went like this. A friend of Darnell's would see him and Jonathan strolling down the side of the road, and would roll to a stop to shout out "Hey." Darnell would lean over to chat through the open window, being just as charming and pleasant as ever, talking about everything and anything except where he was going or why he had a goat with him.

Eventually, the driver would make the standard error in judgment and ask where they were headed. "Oh, just down to The Swing Barn," Darnell would say. "Oh, look at the time. We're a little late and Sue Ten will be really ticked off. Jonathan's her new bouncer."

The driver would take the bait, no matter that Sue Ten had already told Darnell in no uncertain terms that Jonathan was *goat-non-grata*, and Darnell would open the back door to let Jonathan clamber in.

"Now that goat's not going to do anything, is he?" asked the driver.

"Oh, no," said Darnell.

The merry crew would take off, and within a matter of seconds, Jonathan would put his horns up and back through the headliner, take a bite out of the driver's padded neck rest, and/or discharge an impressive supply of pungent pellets and more on the back seat.

Come with me now as we listen for the sound of squealing brakes as the driver stops, evicts his passengers, and then flees the scene.

Of course, Darnell by then is all the closer to his destination, and it's a rare driver who will file a claim for goat damage when he has to admit he was the fool who let the goat into the car in the first place.

My favorite story about Darnell and Jonathan though took place when Darnell was partying in the old Parker place, an abandoned two-story house that had long since lost its paint, windows, and doors, replacing all with spaghnum moss and spiderwebs.

One rainy day, Darnell had decided that it was too wet outside for Jonathan, so he took the goat upstairs and tied his lead to an old bedstead, the kind that the Mummy might have used for afternoon naps, and Darnell headed over here for a piece of strawberry-rhubarb pie and a vanilla milkshake.

Before long, he got into a gin rummy game, and then decided to hit a few balls, and he was coasting along pretty well before someone asked about Jonathan, the way most people might say, "How's the wife and kids?"

Darnell jumped up and headed back down the road to the house. He told me later that he could hear Jonathan bleating long before he could see the goat, hanging out of the second-story window, "holding on by his tippy-toes," as Darnell put it.

I do wish someone had been there with a camera. I know none of us have ever seen Darnell move as fast as he did that day, swooping up the stairs to Jonathan's rescue. I don't know about you, but I do not want to even think about their joyous reunion.

Needless to say, Jonathan is now a first-floor only sort of goat, his hitchhiking days are over, and he does not even have a job. But does Darnell still love him? You bet. Loyalty is one of your second-cousin Darnell's strong points, as much as it scares us all, just a little bit.

Eating Humble Pie

Ever since I took up golf, people have been telling me what a "humbling" sport it is, but I find most of life to be humbling, in one way or another.

Just when I think I'm doing a good deed, and flying rapturously into an imaginary embrace of gratitude, I discover that I am totally off-course, perhaps even in free fall, and I remember that no good deed goes unpunished.

Take, for example, the sad case of the lost-and-found cell phone.

In my not unusual insomniac state the other night, I left my bed, pulled on some clothes, left my turquoise conch cottage around 2:00 a.m., and wandered up the lane to the driving range. A couple of my fellow night-golfers were already there, as usual, and we nodded as we do. No need to talk, just hit a few balls and give sleep another try.

This, as you may understand, is one of the reasons why I am so very glad I have The Morning Guy around, since morning is pretty much foreign territory to me. Ah, but from 2:00 to 4:00 a.m., I know each shadow on the wall by name.

To my delight, I was soon in The Zone, hitting with ease and grace, thinking that maybe one of these days I'll try out something besides a nine iron, but no rush.

I was doing so well, in fact, that I made an error in judgment and sent a gloating text message to The Morning Guy, knowing full well that his phone would be safely turned off, wherever he might be enjoying his vacation.

To my surprise, just a few minutes later a response came in from his phone. That alone was enough to rattle me, but the kicker was that the message—judging by spelling, length, and content—was from a person or persons unknown.

Having lost my place in The Zone, I immersed myself into the problem at hand, and deduced that The Morning Guy's phone had been lost and found, and I quickly cast myself into the fantasy that I was now the heroine who could save the day, and the cell phone, by pulling the strings needed to reunite man and machinery.

Oh, yes. I was giddy with anticipation, delighted to think how happy The Morning Guy would be with me; so happy, in fact, that he might even give me that long-promised up-close-and-personal golf lesson.

Unfortunately, by the time I did make contact with him, I was not only wildly tired, but also a bit light-headed from living so comfortably in the future, and I'd totally discounted how upset he might possibly be about the lost phone.

In the real world, all I had to do was say, "Someone found your phone. Here's the number to call," and I would have been good to go. But I was so damn busy giving myself a really nice, shiny medal for tracking him down out of town and far away—which was certainly far from easy—that when it came time to deliver the news, my words were sadly both sarcastic and silly, thereby canceling out both my effort and my intent.

His somber response was to inform me that "my fun at his expense" was not fun to him.

Ay yi yi!

I fell to Earth in a heap, and I have been banging my head against the pie-shop wall ever since.

All I can do now is to eat the mandatory slice of humble pie, the traditional meal of those who must learn through experience how to act submissively and apologetically, especially when admitting to an error.

I don't mind the metaphor of humble pie, and it seems fine and appropriate, but I'm not too wild about the real origin of the phrase.

In England in the 1500s, the name used for deer entrails, liver, and heart was numbles, or possibly noumbles, nomblys, or even noubles; a hundred years later the term had morphed to a more uniform "umbles," which were in fact a common pie ingredient.

Even Samuel Pepys, a notorious blogger, was known to enjoy a bit of umble pie, as stated in his blog on July 5, 1662: "I having some venison given me a day or two ago, and so I had a shoulder roasted, another baked, and the umbles baked in a pie, and all very well done."

At the same time, the word humble came into play, meaning "of lowly rank" or "having a low estimate of oneself," and before long the two terms merged, giving us the current concept of behind the phrase "eating humble pie."

Interestingly, if you are a fan of pie history as am I, humble pie has followed the path of mince pie and turned itself from a simple meat dish into a tasty and sweet fruit dish. Now, if I were one to stretch metaphors even more than I already did, you might be seeing a happy ending to this story, and I hope you are.

Time will tell if I have survived this particular meal, but keep reading for a recipe to put us both on the right path.

Humble Pie Recipe

Prepare an unbaked pie shell
Prepare a filling made from

> 3 large sweet apples, peeled and cut into small pieces
> 1 1/2 C of fresh cranberries
> 1 C light brown sugar
> Place filling into pie shell.
> Mix up following ingredients and sprinkle on top of the apple-cranberry filling.
> 3/4 C finely chopped walnuts
> 1/4 C light brown sugar
> 1/4 C flour
> 3 T softened butter
> Cinnamon, nutmeg & ginger to taste
> Pinch of salt

Bake in a 425-degree oven for 20 minutes.
Cover pie with foil and turn oven down to 350 degrees.
Bake another 30 minutes.

Serve with excessive humility.
Apologize as much as necessary to make yourself feel better.

I'll tell you when you can stop.

Yoga Retreat Golf Meditation

"Focus," he says, "on a faraway sound."
Instructed well, I still listen instead
for the silence just beyond the sounds
of the Costa Rican rain forest:
the stream, the wind, the birds, the dogs.

I listen as always for the perfect click
of the well-placed stroke
lofting a ball, somewhere yet
behind the silence that hovers
between the birds and the monkeys
and the rain forest sky.

Not far from here, in the deep dark serenity
a billboard blocks out the pasture
strewn with perfectly lean
cattle—and shade.

I'm listening for silence but seeing the billboard
promising beaches, promising golf.

Or promising sand traps and pain,
I'm not quite sure which,
and I have quite enough pain
already in shoulders and spine and in knees.

I'm listening for silence
but drifting myself
into a turqouise-striped beach chair
striped canvas above me,
an umbrella in my drink that maybe
is rum in a wild carved-out pineapple
or maybe straight rum in a souvenir glass.

You, of course, are there with me,
contented, relaxed.

I'm listening for silence
but I'm swinging my club
seeing perfection, simplicity, ease.

I hope I remember
what my body can do
when I come out of the rain forest
and back to the lights
where I can listen for silence
behind the sounds
of the driving range at night.

Then maybe I'll hear
the song that you're humming
behind the silence that hovers
between the birds and the lizards
and the Florida sky.

Four and Twenty Blackbirds

Life has been pretty hectic this week at The Slice of Heaven 24-Hour Pie Shop and Driving Range. I am still catching up after taking some time off to go to a yoga retreat in Costa Rica. Ideally, the balance skills and core strength that I am learning in my yoga practice will ultimately pay off for me in a better golf game, or at least in balance and core strength. Period.

Now I'm having to fill in for The Morning Guy while he is on vacation, and that means actually getting up in the morning. I'll admit that I've been very spoiled in that regard, but I'll be fine. I have some excellent notes here about how to restock the soda machine, notes which I will immediately pass on to Sparkle Junior and your second-cousin Darnell.

Personally, I'll be busy working on plans for the Pie Museum, and I know you are looking forward to the day when that opens, although you might well wish we'd get to work on the putting green first. Perhaps we will.

I already hit a snag in trying to find out about that "Four and Twenty Blackbirds Baked in a Pie" nursery rhyme. It seems that there are a number of stories about what the words really mean, if anything at all. As I read through the possibilities, I definitely found myself leaning toward the Blackbeard the Pirate version, because it is entertaining if nothing else.

Sadly, the idea that "Four and Twenty Blackbirds" was some kind of pirate code was actually concocted by the folks at Snopes.com as an example of "False Authority Syndrome," in which they pretty nicely prove that we are all fairly gullible folk.

I was disappointed, because I like pretty much any combination of pirates and pie (or golf and pie), and I had hoped the story was true. In fact, I'd already pictured one helluva nice display for the museum, including a signed copy of Tim Powers' fantastic book *On Stranger Tides*, which should definitely be on The Pie Shop bookshelves by now.

If you haven't read it yet, I'll consider lending one of my copies to you, but plan on paying a hefty deposit before you take the book out of my sight.

I did, though, find some other references to the four-and-twenty which were interesting, although a bit of a downturn after the pirate possibility, but how do you like this? A 1549 Italian cookbook does, in fact, contain a recipe "to make pies so that birds may be alive in them and flie out when it is cut up."

Or am I just falling victim to False Authority Syndrome again?

If you know any more about this particular historical pie, do let me know. Check your copy of *The Annotated Mother Goose*, too. There might be something there.

The Slice of Heaven

Michel Ten

Your second-cousin Darnell has been talking about starting a horse-and-buggy tour of the neighborhood as a way to "support the community," he says. Or a way to boondoogle the few tourists that we get out here so close the 'Glades, I say.

"Just what will you cover on this tour?" I want to know. "Once you've gone by The Pie Shop, The Driving Range, The Swing Barn, and Pancho Villas, what's left? The bonsai forest?"

Darnell seemed a little puzzled by my lack of enthusiasm, which was tempered by the knowledge that he did not have a horse nor a buggy, and he sauntered off to The Swing Barn to see if he might have better luck with Sue Ten.

I suspect that she probably gave him comments very similar to mine, with perhaps a bit less diplomacy and tact, two qualities which I am seriously trying to develop.

I do actually like the idea of the buggy ride, but I think there has to be an audience for it first, not unlike The Village Players recent production of The Mikado, in which Sue Ten had a staring role. Sadly, most of the people who were interested in hearing Gilbert and Sullivan were already in the cast, so that left but few of us to fill the seats.

Still, we all had a good time, especially during Sue Ten's encore, for which she sang the song "Frank Mills," from *Hair*. The fact that she was still in her geisha costume made it all the more endearing, since her outfit gave the song more of a Teeny-Bopper Butterfly flavor.

Speaking of horse-and-buggy rides, Sue and I have been trying to figure out if Michel Ten, whom I met in Havana, could possibly be a relative, but we weren't able to find a family line from here to there, so chances are that the similarity in names was either a coincidence or a misunderstanding.

Little Peach and I met Michel on our second day in Havana as we strolled past the horse-cabs. We were besieged by the drivers, a fairly raucous and noisy crew of men in crisp pastel-plaid cotton shirts and jeans. They were all cheery and optimistic that we would take them up on their tour offers, but we had already signed up for our bus tour, so we continued our stroll down the Prado.

Michel, bless his heart, proceeded to stroll with us, spewing his spiel, still, about how great his particular buggy tour would be. Little Peach took him aside for a moment and explained that we were in Havana without luggage or a change of clothing, and what we really wanted to know was where we could pick up a little dress or two, cheap. We also wanted such niceties as deodorant and shampoo.

None of that really stumped him, but we learned from him that most if not all the retail shops in Cuba were closed for Liberation Day, so with or without him, we would not be able to do too much shopping. We continued our walk, without Michel Ten, and admired the buildings along the Prado, and the young skateboarders operating mainly with lengths of wood and old roller-skate wheels.

Before we parted company, though, Michel Ten did warn us, "Those bus tours aren't any good. You should come with me. If you change your mind, just ask for Michel Ten. That's me."

We asked his price, shook our heads, and said good-bye. When we returned to our hotel a few hours later, Michel was still out in the square, working his work, as charming as ever.

That afternoon, we did go on the bus tour, where we met The Philosopher Detective and did have a pleasant afternoon and evening, but we both had to admit we could not always understand our tour guide, and Little Peach did not have an opportunity to ask the detailed questions for which she is so well known, and perhaps a little feared by tour guides everywhere.

The next morning, I told her, "I think we should go talk to Michel Ten and see if we can get him to come down on his price."

We had a wonderful full breakfast in the elegant old dining room of the Hotel Inglaterra, admiring the tile work from days gone by and the contemporary painting of Cuba today. We chatted with the staff, sipped our juices and coffees, and smiled at the thought of where we really were, with luggage or without. Then, we went out to find Michel Ten.

Of course, he was not there, and several other horse-cab drivers claimed to be him. We said, "No, no, no." Then they started to call from one to the other, "Michel! Michel Ten!" until suddenly he appeared, a great smile on his face.

We proceeded to make our offer for a cheaper ride, but he looked sad and said it could not be done. "You see that man over there? That is my boss. I must give him the price." Little Peach and I suggested a shorter ride. He said no. And, great negotiators that we are, we said, "Okay, let's go."

I had forgotten that at some point I had tried to teach one of the other drivers how to sing "Una Paloma Blanca," and as we began to pull away in our cab drawn by Michel Ten's little horse Mulatta, that driver jumped up on the side of the cab and sang for us, getting the first line out perfectly, and then faking it after that—just as I had. Michel shooed him away, and we took off on our slow, relaxing tour, with Little Peach asking every question that came into her mind, and Michel Ten doing his best to answer them in his almost-perfect English.

One word that he did have trouble with, though, was "horse," which he pronounced as "whore."

We ignored that at first, until he got into an explanation of memorial statues of soldiers on horseback, and what it means if "the whore has all four feet on the ground" as opposed to "the whore has two feet on the ground."

"I think you mean to say 'horse' said Little Peach, emphasizing the "s" at the end. "Oh!" said Michel. "So what does 'whore' mean?"

I said "puta" and Little Peach said "prostitute" and then we all laughed, and continued our journey past Morro Castle, the open-air market, the booksellers, the museums, the Spanish Embassy, and more until we reached the bar where Michel promised us the best mojitos in Cuba.

We each had one, at 11:00 a.m., and then with cups in hand, continued our tour, which ended up lasting at least 90 minutes of main attractions, side streets, and vignettes of daily life in Havana. Was it better than the bus tour? Absolutely.

Was drinking mojitos before noon a good idea? Perhaps not, especially since we continued to drink Bucanero at lunch and through the afternoon, until the time that we decided to ride on the top of the double-decker hop-on-hop-off bus, our cans of beer neatly tucked into the drink holders.

As the bus sped past the horse-cab area, we stood up and yelled, "Michel! Michel Ten!" but I do not know if he heard us. If you ever go to Havana, please look up Michel 10. I have his phone number, and I'm sure he'd love to hear from you. Tell him that Una Paloma Blanca sent you.

The Slice of Heaven

The Caddy

Most of the guys who hang out at The Slice of Heaven 24-Hour Pie Shop and Driving Range know that I don't take direction well, and they are happy to let me take my golf lessons from Sandra, safely off the premises, and to let me wrestle my golf tips out of The Morning Guy, when he feels like sharing.

Anyone new on the scene also usually can tell within minutes that I am better off left alone, determined student of the swing that I am.

Last night, we were surprisingly low on customers, but the weather was slightly cool and damp, and perhaps a few people were still out celebrating the results of the recent presidential election. I know that Sandra was, and Sue Ten was still cranking out red-white-and-blue cupcakes for customers over at The Swing Barn.

I didn't mind having the extra space to myself, and I nodded to people as they came through The Pie Shop door to sit at the picnic tables with their pumpkin pie and hot coffee before loading up their buckets and starting to play.

I was doing pretty well, and was fairly pleased, so I didn't fully notice that someone was teeing up in the space just behind me. Suddenly, the tide changed, and my next shot went completely backward, just a few inches off the ground, and abruptly knocked the other player's ball right off the tee.

He jumped away in surprise, and soon commenced to announce that he had never seen such a shot in his life, not after teaching golf for two and a half decades, not after playing in innumerable tournaments, not after a lifetime in which golf was pretty much the primary focus.

"My God!" he said. "You couldn't do that again in a million years." I begged to differ. My shots have a fiercely wild variety, but he was convinced that he had already seen me in a nice rhythm, hitting balls with no trouble.

"Yes," he said. "I came out and wondered where I should play. I looked around and saw you were doing your thing, and I thought, 'That's fine. That lady is hitting some nice shots, so she won't need any advice and I can just get in my practice with no problem.'"

After that pronouncement, he proceeded to watch me, which made both of us and a couple of other people nervous as well.

Finally, neither he nor the next guy in the line could stand to see me send one more ball scuttling down the grass, and they both commenced to give me more tips in 10 minutes than The Morning Guy had given me all year, only their tips were not written down in perfect block lettering on Post-It notes for me to refer to later.

By then, they could see that I was taking on that deer-in-the-headlights look, and they backed off, but not for long. Try this! Try that! It made me think of Thing One and Thing Two in the *Cat in the Hat* books. Sparkle was so fascinated by the scene that he came out on the pretense of picking up buckets so he would smirk at close range. Knowing I was distracted, he told several people to go ahead and re-shoot any balls were lying close by.

Why not?

I'll have to admit, that ploy did soon disperse the crowd although I don't know why. They can shoot all the balls they want, anyway, but I guess there seemed to be some bargain-basement mentality at work there.

Soon I was left with only one critic, and he was a bit of a bulldog about the whole thing. He picked up the wood that I usually lay on the ground just to help me keep some sense of alignment and said, "This club is getting all dirty, this is no good. Why don't you like this club? It's a nice one."

I said it was too big, and besides that I like my nine iron and don't really need another club right now. For some reason, this concept always reminds me of my mother teaching herself to knit using Christmas string. I don't fully know why.

He shook his head. "Go ahead," he said. "Try this one," and he handed me the wood. I tried, I failed, and he proceeded to offer corrections, including the usual Keep Your Head Down, which I thought I had been doing. Apparently not. I may never lift my head again after last night, though.

Then I hit a few more, and did all right, but still hit too high up on the ball. This has never been a concern for me since I have never been in any rush to learn the game. After all, I live here. The meter is not running, and I have an endless bucket of balls.

For the next hour, this guy—who turns out to be a professional caddy—continued to advise, tweak, talk, demonstrate, cajole, and advise again, taking the occasional breath to comment that he just couldn't seem to stop himself since I was so close to hitting a really fine shot. Then the Caddy also told me to stop doing some girlie stuff. Excuse me?

Next The Caddy starting pulling clubs out of his bag to see if I could do better with one of them, until he completely lost all sense of judgment and turned his shiny blue featherweight driver over to me. I swear, I felt like Christopher, one of the mini-Tiger-Woods kids who runs around here with a club bigger than he is, but I loved it. I backed away, I swung, and I heard that satisfying metallic clink, and I did not look up . . . at least not until the ball was well on its way.

I did look at The Caddy and said, "Thanks. I do believe I owe you a piece of pie," and I headed inside.

Oddly enough, The Caddy, this guy who had talked non-stop by then for almost two hours, became strangely quiet without a golf club in his hands. And that was fine, too. We both needed a break.

I just can't wait now for my next official lesson with Sandra so I can find out if I retained any new skills, or if I just went into sensory overload.

I should probably take her some pie, too.

Will Work for Pie

I'm sorry to say that I have not been able to keep up with Pie Shop chores as well as I expected with The Morning Guy gone on his vacation, although vacation might not be the right word for it. Let's just say "during his absence." So, I was understandably relieved then when I saw a guy out the I-95 access ramp, holding a sign that said, "Will work for pie."

Now, some may say it's risky business to bring a stranger in to one's place of business, but I say, "Damn, man. He's willing to work for pie." Even The Morning Guy wants pie, ice cream, coffee, and free golf. This new guy is a bargain. I will, however, take your warnings under consideration, but first let's see how much pie he can eat.

My son Chandler and I have both had odd experiences with panhandlers in the past. I still remember being asked for money for food by a young denizen of the streets in Denver.

I was hesitant to talk to him since I could see my bus approaching, but I decided to open my heart and I reached into my capacious bag and pulled out my lunch to share, remembering how one of my undergrad profs had done that for me on more than one occasion.

I handed over my tuna fish sandwich, but to my surprise, the scruffy young man did not thank me. No, he held the skimpy lightweight baggie up to the light, as if expecting to see something revelatory on the bread, perhaps the image of Lord Vader. I don't know.

"What's in this?" he asked.

"Tuna, mayo, a little relish."

"Relish?"

"Yes. Relish. Are you hungry or not? If you don't want the sandwich, I'll take it back."

He thought it over and kept the sandwich, by which time I had missed my bus. I watched him scuttle off, still sniffing the baggie, and poking his finger into the pristine white bread.

I waited to climb on the next bus. Starting to feel a little hungry myself, I got on, sat down, and discovered that someone had left his or her lunch on the seat. Sure enough, it was a tuna fish sandwich, plus a second baggie with six Oreo cookies in it. Score! I came out ahead on that one.

My son Chandler, one of the twins, told me once that he had been in process of moving and had a lot of cupboard-cleanout stuff in his car, and decided to hand those groceries over to a guy who regularly camped out by the side of the road.

This camper was not an especially good beggar, but a persistent one, and probably by the end of the day, he would have collected enough coinage and low-end swag to get him through the night.

When Chandler arrived at his new digs, however, he discovered that he still had the bag of groceries in his car, so what had he given the panhandler? An extensive collection of cookie cutters and pastry tools. He drove back to the highway, somewhat relieved that our man was still there, and made a swap, not without being soundly scolded for improper gifting.

Apparently, cookie cutters—no matter how festive or celebratory—are not what most panhandlers are seeking.

We are both now a little more cautious and careful now about what we hand out to strangers on the road, or on the sidewalk. Still, I have a weakness for someone who will work for pie, and when my new friend and I reached The Pie Shop, I got out my to-do list while he had some quiche lorraine and coffee for breakfast.

Sparkle told me that Sue Ten was on the phone, so I stopped to speak to her for a few minutes, during which the new guy moved on to a plate of deep-dish apple pie with cheese. I told Sue Ten I would talk to her later, and said, "I'm getting the cabinet doors fixed," to which she replied "It's about time."

She had an unfortunate experience in my conch cottage one day. I was in my rocker out on the porch and heard her yelp with surprise when one of my cabinet doors came off right in her hand, because the screws in the hinges were missing.

"Oh," I said. "That one. I never use that one. The screws in the hinges are missing. What were you looking for?"

She said she was looking for cake plates—like I have those!—and ended up just bringing her whole cake out to the porch with two forks, a quart of milk, and two Mason jars.

"You should get that cabinet fixed. It's just a couple of screws."

"I know."

"You need to call a plumber about the faucet in your bathroom, too."

"I know."

"The broken mini-blinds in your bedroom are atrocious."

"I know."

"How do you like the cake?"

"It's wonderful."

And it was: Lemon cake with chocolate fudge frosting, my birthday dish of choice for many years. Remembering that combination of flavors, I started flipping through my recipe file looking for a lemon chiffon recipe with chocolate-cookie crumb crust, when I saw the new guy's empty plate. I wasn't really ready to tackle the cabinets yet, so I slid over some chocolate-pecan-bourbon pie, and looked at my list again.

Maybe this guy could help me bring some more books up from the cottage and put them on the new pie-shop shelves. Joe Sparkle Junior had already restocked the soda machine and was out on the E-Z Cart slowly, meticulously scooping up golf balls. While I was reviewing the list, I noticed that someone had left an unfinished crossword puzzle on the counter, so I started to ink in a few entries.

The new guy finished off another cup of coffee, and smiled. I gave him a piece of banana cream pie with extra whipped cream and he went right to work on that, while I finished the puzzle and looked over my latest crop of Post-It notes, realizing that each one was a project in the making, not something to be tampered with by rank amateurs, such as the new guy and me.

He finished his pie, and I said, "I think we're good. One for the road?" He nodded, and I wrapped up a slice of blueberry cheesecake for him, then we headed out to the highway again. I dropped him off where I found him, and gave him $20 for his time.

When I got back, I parked at The Pie Shop and walked down the lane to my cottage, where I noticed that Sue Ten's bike was on my porch and the light was on in the kitchen. I approached quietly to peek in the window, but she wouldn't have heard me anyway over the whirring sound of the cordless screwdriver as she patiently replaced the missing screws.

I walked back up the lane, and started fixing some steak and mushroom pie for her supper. I don't know what I would do without her. Seriously. Not that many people are willing to work for pie.

Chocolate-Laced Lemon Chiffon Pie

First, prepare a chocolate-cookie pie crust, and set it aside
Assemble your ingredients:

>1/4 oz unflavored gelatin
>1 1/2 C sugar
>6T water
>6 eggs
>dash salt
>3/4 C fresh lemon juice
>1 1/2 t grated lemon peel
>2 oz semi-sweet chocolate
>1 1/2 T butter
>1 1/2 C whipping cream

Dissolve the gelatin and 3/4 C sugar in hot water in the top of a double boiler or in a microwave-safe bowl.

When ingredients are fully dissolved, wait for mixture to cool before continuing.

Separate the eggs and beat the yolks into the cooled gelatin mixture.

Add salt and lemon juice.

Simmer for five minutes, stirring repeatedly, until mixture becomes thick.

Add lemon peel, then chill. Take your time. No hurry, no worry.

Meanwhile, whip up the egg whites, adding 3/4C sugar, until the whites form peaks.

Whip the cream, too.

Fold the egg whites, the cream, and the gelatin mixture in together, and go back to chilling until it all reaches a nice level of firmness.

Melt the butter and semi-sweet chocolate.

Bring out the pie crust and start scooping the filling into it, alternating the filling with drizzled chocolate.

Do this three times, ending with a lacy drizzled pattern over the top.

If you run out of chocolate drizzle, just make some more.

Have fun.

Full Moon Ramble

Some of us went to the beach for a full moon picnic last night, and I've got to say, it was an exceptionally pleasant time, away from the bright lights of the driving range, the muted noise of the dancers and drinkers at The Swing Barn, and the endless to-do list at The Slice of Heaven Pie Shop.

Looking up at that wonderful bright moon, I thought of the nights when I've watched it come up over the driving range, rising above the trees. One night in particular, it was fascinating because as the moon came up, the raccoons came out, and a number of the guys had a little fun in shooting their golf balls at the furry moving targets, who responded by moving just a little bit faster.

I've never been a big fan of raccoons, so I did enjoy watching the target practice. The twins probably still remember when our kitchen in Maine was taken over by raccoons, who seemed quite angry that we were up in the night trying to make them move out. Eventually, the critters lumbered up the stairs and out a third-floor window, but for a while, it was really touch and go.

Then, in Missouri, in our little house by the big lake, we watched a whole family of raccoons, plus their realtor, check out a big old dead tree within sight of our porch, but once they saw us, they decided the neighborhood did not meet their standards, and they moved along.

Snubbed by raccoons! Oh, man, that hurt.

Of course, the full moon does provide another excuse for me to talk about golf, pie, and the universe. As you recall, NASA once did have a plan to put the first apple pie on the moon, and Alan Shepard was the first man to play golf on the moon, so by now it must all be coming together for you. Add to this, a lovely sentiment expressed by Carl Sagan, "If you want to make an apple pie from scratch, you must first create the universe."

Now, you could take that to mean that only God can create a pie, but I'll interpret it in broader terms to remind myself that golf, pie, the moon, and Alan Shepard are all part of the same grand plan. My question of late has been what type of apples to use in my Alan Shepard Pie, so I checked out the harvest list for an orchard near Shepard's old home town of Derry, New Hampshire.

I was delighted to see so many choices: Jerseymac, Tydeman, Paulared, Burgundy, Gingergold, Jonamac, McIntosh, Gala, Cortland, Empire, Honeycrisp, Macoun, Red Delicious, Jonagold, Golden Delicious, and Mutsu. I tell you, the sky's the limit. Just reading the list of apples sounds like poetry to me, and more and more, I suspect that poetry will be the form that Alan Shepard Pie takes, once I finally create it as something to be consumed under the full moon on the golf course of your choosing.

One likely place may be McInnis Park, just 20 minutes from the Golden Gate Bridge. Two nights ago the Golf Center there hosted night golf with special guest Michael Murphy, author of the Shivas Irons books, which are my particular favorites. I came across this news while browsing through the Shivas Irons Society website, which I recommend to you because Shivas Irons fans do so completely understand the metaphor of golf.

That's all for now, my dear. I hope we can talk again soon. Don't forget to send me your golf tips, and I'll keep a pie on the windowsill just for you.

Night Golf Flu Shot Clinic

I think sometimes more people would understand the mystical nature of golf if the game were less accessible. I mean really, drive down any given road in SoFLA, and before you know it, you'll find yourself passing a golf course, or two, or three. Some are behind high hedges, but for the most part they are right there, waiting to lure you in.

At least, here at The Slice of Heaven 24-Hour Pie Shop and Driving Range, we are so far off the beaten path that when you come to us, you bring along a sense of deliberation and destination, and I like that about our visitors. Except, of course, for my ex-husband Pretty Boy Boyd, they tend not to do much by accident.

It always bothered me when Boyd would arrive home lit up like one of those impossible-to-blow-out candles that are so funny to everyone except for the birthday boy or girl.

Boyd liked to say, by way of apology for whatever distress he was about to bestow on me, "I didn't mean to get so drunk." What did he think was going to happen once he started pouring pints of Guinness down his throat?

It was hardly worth discussing. Boyd, as far as I can tell, just likes to go through life in a state of chronic surprise. Even now, I can see the look of mystification on his face as he finds himself parked outside The Swing Barn in my old Toyota.

Pretty soon, though, he'll remember his recent encounter with our resident feral green iguana, and he'll leave again. That iguana has proven to be much more effective than a more traditional restraining order.

Most people, like you, come here by choice or obligation, rarely by chance, and that holds true for Nurse Crotchett, too. I hadn't seen her since the Hollywood Halloween party, and tonight I was surprised to discover that she really is a nurse.

For the party, she'd worn a snug white uniform complete with cap, white stockings, and shoes, but now she is in lavender scrubs with matching eye shadow, and she is carrying a clipboard as well as a medical bag.

"Where do you want me to set up?" she asks. Quick as ever, all I can say is, "What?"

"For your flu-shot clinic," she says, handing me a typed memo, on my letterhead, recommending that we participate in the county's "Alternate Hours" flu-shot program.

"Oh, yes," I say, noting The Morning Guy's name on the bottom of the memo, vaguely remembering seeing a green Post-It note that said "Flu Shots Tuesday Night" stuck to my computer monitor.

Crotchett efficiently commandeered one of The Pie Shop tables, and I took her some coffee and a piece of blackberry-raisin pie. Within minutes, your second-cousin Darnell was there, filling out paperwork, handing over eight dollars, and rolling up his sleeve for his shot.

I saw more cars pulling up, and called Joe Sparkle Junior in from the driving range to help with the influx of customers, considerably more than we normally have rolling in at 11:00 p.m.

During one of the lulls, Crotchett told me that all-night flu-shot clinics were definitely unusual in this part of the world, but a recent *New York Times* article had given The Morning Guy the idea to run one here, and her boss at the county public health office wanted to be seen as an innovator, so we were the test case.

I will say, it was actually quite pleasant to have so many people around, and most of them did stay on well after the pinch of the Crotchett's needle had passed. We went through more than a dozen servings of blackberry-raisin, 20 of banana cream, seven of midnight chocolate, and two of pumpkin-cheesecake.

Because we were so busy inside The Pie Shop, I didn't notice that the driving range lights were acting up again. Finally, someone came in and said, "Just turn them off. The strobing is giving Darnell flashbacks." I pulled the switch and came back inside, leaving a note for The Morning Guy to check on the problem, and thinking the range would empty out.

I was wrong. There were still a dozen golfers out there in the dim glow of The Pie Shop lights, hitting balls as well as usual, if not better. In fact, freed from seeing the arc or the final distance, all they could do was concentrate on the swing, and that seemed to be to their advantage.

I joined them, closing my eyes since there was really nothing to see except the distant glow of the porch light down at my little turquoise conch cottage. Like the rest of the line, I hit the ball anyway, telling by the sound whether the hit was good or not. All in all, I found it to be a most satisfying experience.

Throughout the rest of the night, people continued to make the deliberate drive out to the edge of the 'Glades for flu shots, pie, and mystical golf in the dark.

Finally, I saw the light in the east, and I went inside to say good-night to Crotchett, but she was already gone. I glanced out the front door and saw The Morning Guy just pulling in on his motorcycle, counting the cars, as he strolled around to the side door to begin his day, as I ended my night.

I picked up a piece of quiche, nodded to Sparkle, and headed down the lane to my cottage, satisfied, happy, and pleased that I would not have to go into town for my flu shot this year.

Mississippi

I haven't had any particular song stuck in my head for a while, but tonight I found myself repeating lyrics from Bob Dylan's "Mississippi" out on the driving range. I can't say that it helped or hurt me, but when I got back inside I did stop to listen to a few different versions. The lines that kept rolling around tonight were:

I was raised in the country, I been workin' in the town
I've been in trouble ever since I set my suitcase down

I don't really know why those surfaced, except that this past week, I do feel like I've been in a bit of trouble, and haven't really understood why. As far as I know, all I did was to set my suitcase down. Well, sometimes that happens to us all. I'm saddened by the folks who have gone on the defensive around me. I suspect this is the sad effect of that waning gibbous moon that I keep warning you about.

Anyway, I love the Dylan version, but if you stop in at The Pie Shop, you'll see we have the Dixie Chicks one on the jukebox, and this is the one I'm hearing tonight. I'd forgotten about another line, "I'm going to look at you until my eyes goes blind."

Ah, yes.

Once I felt that way about my ex-husband Pretty Boy Boyd, but that was a long time ago. As I listen to the lyrics to this song, I've got to say, I love them all: "Stick with me baby, stick with me anyhow. Things should start to get interesting right about now."

Speaking of romance, a lot has happened since we last spoke. The big news is that both Sue Ten and your second-cousin Darnell tell me that they have seen The Morning Guy out on what appears to be a date. I find this news to be both appalling and beguiling at the same time.

As you may recall, one of the guests at our Hollywood Halloween party was dressed as a Stepford Wife, and she caught our hero's eye when none of the rest of us even knew he was there. Surprisingly, we now learn, her costume and demeanor were no ruse at all since she is a throw-back to the Mirabel Morgan "Total Woman" days, and she has had years (some might say decades) in which to practice her craft. Her real costume was the addition of a Stepford Husband, whom we now know was actually her cousin Henry from Ann Arbor.

I still don't have all the details of this new development, but apparently The Morning Guy was so smitten that he actually spoke to her, obtained her name and phone number, and within days had called her for a date. This information, too, may explain why he was so upset the night he lost his cell phone since he had trusted that wily technology to keep the two of them in touch while he was out of town on his vacation.

According to Sue Ten, the happy couple has now had several meals together at The Swing Barn, and Sue observes that Steppie always orders her pastrami sandwich and fries with extra coleslaw. Then she eats half the sandwich and the coleslaw, leaving the rest of the sandwich and the fries for The Morning Guy. He smiles. She smiles. He talks. She listens. We are all quite anxious to see how this romance will progress.

Last seen, Steppie was dressed as a cheerleader for The Morning Guy's favorite college football team, and they were tossing back Yuenglings and pickled eggs with no concern about gastric after affects, but she never lost track of the score, and she apparently has an encyclopedic knowledge of the game.

24-Hour Pie Shop and Driving Range

Meanwhile, I have been thinking a lot lately about the whole concept of matchmaking and matches in general. I do love my life here at The Slice of Heaven 24-Hour Pie Shop and Driving Range, especially my freedom to be as frivolous or as serious as I want to be, but from time to time, I do think it might be nice to go dancing with a willing partner on a Friday night.

When Nurse Crotchett was on site for our Flu Shot Clinic, she encouraged me to try out an Internet dating service, eHarmony. "It's free this weekend," she said. "Free."

I gave it a try, passing a few hours of insomnia answering pages and pages about myself, my attitudes, my preferences, and so on. On each page, I read the disclaimer that there were no wrong answers. "Of course not," I thought. "Besides, I certainly feel that I am giving out the right answers." Finally, I got to the end, and told the machine to begin searching for my match.

"Geographical area?" it asked. "Why limit it?" I thought, and went for this option: "Anywhere in the World." An additional question asked me "How important is this geographical area?" I said, "Very." I may be open minded, but I'm not sure I'm ready to date extra-terrestrials, at least not just yet.

The screen assured me that the eHarmony system was searching, searching, searching its 85,000-member database. Finally I received my results: "Our matching system was not able to find any matches for you."

Hello? No matches anywhere in the world?

Sue Ten, on hearing this news, just shook her head. "I can only imagine what foolishness you put down on that form. Next time, you should let me fill it out for you." Both my kids assured me that eHarmoney was funded by the religious right and was no place for a good Unitarian-Univesalist Taoist Pagan such as myself to be looking for a date for the New Years Eve festivities at The Swing Barn.

Perhaps I am just matchless. Or maybe it takes someone very special, like you, to appreciate me and my little quirks. Perhaps Sue Ten is right, and I should not list *Fight Club* as my favorite movie, or *Hedwig and the Angry Inch* as my favorite musical. But that would not be authentic.

I do love Hedwig. My life is so easy compared to hers, and "The Origin of Love" moves me, so would I really want to spend New Years Eve with someone who cared not for her, or for Tyler Durden, for that matter? Get real. Or watch it yourself and tell me what you think.

Perhaps also I should not mention insomnia, pie, or how many golf balls I hit in the course of any single week or single night. And perhaps I should have mentioned that I do love to wear high heels and lingerie, but I didn't really see any place where I would include that detail. Ah, well.

The language of love is never easy to learn. Take, for example, the sweet note that I found in a copy of *Leslie Nielsen's Stupid Little Golf Book* at the local Goodwill. I think the note's author Buddy was faking his interest in golf, but he did show his sincere interest in Lillian. Still that's often not enough—or else it leads to stalking and that's no good at all.

As for the book itself, I'll add it to The Pie Shop bookshelves, and maybe I'll leave the note tucked in as a bookmark, too. I hate to break up a set.

Cinderella's Pumpkin Pie

Consistently friendly and untempermental,
Cinderella never asked for much.

She told me her life too often was filled
with flavorless spice
and not that honest pumpkin flavor
that only princes recognize.

So, she learned how to sweeten the pie
without masking the taste
of fields full of orange
and fall festivals held on old village greens.

The secret she told me is in the milk,
sweetened, condensed,
ready to go
into a filling
both intense and sweet—
yet never high in fat.

Two whole eggs, two yolks,
the least grainy filling,
silky smooth,
served best in a glass slipper.

"But, my dear," I asked,

"with the pumpkin pureed for your pie,
how will you get to the ball?"

"I'd rather stay honest," she said,
"and be who I am."

"Besides," she continued,
"the pumpkin aroma will be quite enough,
to bring him my way,
and then I will serve up
ambrosia for him,
a dessert plate for me,
and always a slice left for you."

I Am Not My Brother's Driver

Last night, I fell just a little bit in love with a couple of guys who came in late and stayed later. It was about 2:00 a.m., and my new apprentice Prentiss seemed to have everything in The Pie Shop under control.

She's already mastered the fine art of making a light flaky vodka pie crust, and I'm sure her Key lime pie filling will be the tops after a few more practice sessions. At any rate, I'm glad to have her here, especially now that The Morning Guy is spending so much time with his Stepford Girlfriend. She doesn't have them wearing matching outfits, yet, but I'm sure it won't be long.

I've been away, visiting the twins and touring museums, getting a lot of great new ideas for our own pie museum, which we'll start working on as soon as Sparkle Junior makes a bit more progress with the putting green. At some point, he will need to stop studying the blue prints and get to work with the Bobcat. We are all looking forward to that.

I enjoyed my travels immensely, but missed having the time and opportunity to practice my swing, so I was happy to be outside under the lights, greeting the range iguanas and raccoons once again. As usual, it took me about 20 swings to have any sense of timing or balance at all, but then I hit a few good ones, and felt some semblance of confidence in my stoke.

I hadn't noticed the new guys on the range, but then I started hearing a soft voice behind me, giving a running commentary, and punctuated with the occasional "whoo hoo" and "that'll play!" I looked to see who was there, and saw that my new companion was a

6'5" African American man with a big smile, a diamond earring, and a 46" titanium driver.

"What do you think? This is my brother's club," he said, pointing at an equally tall but considerably more slender guy a few spots down to my right.

I told him it looked like a pretty good club to me.

"Oh it is," he said. "He spends a lot of money on his golf clubs, and this is certainly a fine one, but you know what. It's not my club." He nodded and went back to hitting balls, and talking to himself.

For the next hour, I felt privileged to be included in the banter between the two brothers, tuned in to the sound of their swings, and I enjoyed watching their golf balls fly to the far boundary of the range. Most of all, I liked the sheer joy that I felt around them, their openness with each other, and with anyone else who wanted to chat for a while.

"I came to golf late, but my son plays now," he said with pride, "and this game will put him through school just like football did for me."

My friend The Caddy came by to offer me his usual litany of tips, and the brothers just told him I was doing fine. "Are you trying to teach her to play?" marveled the brother on my left. "You should know better than that."

I liked that observation, just as I liked the guy's understanding that his brother might have "better" clubs, but the best ones for him were his own. They say that true wealth comes from having "enough," and it was a treat to meet someone who made that real for me. I hope you, too, will always have enough, but be sure to save some room for dessert.

The *Cosmo* Quiz

Yesterday, to my surprise, there was no Post-It note from The Morning Guy on my computer screen. Instead, his Stepford Girlfriend was bustling around tidying-up my stacks of file folders, catalogs, and return-reply envelopes.

Once I pointed out that all that clutter was solely my concern, and a very small concern at that, she smiled sweetly, grabbed a piece of raspberry cream pie, and settled down to read her copy of the *Cosmo Compendium of 812,683 Ways To Please Your Man*.

I resisted the urge to point out that the book was actually a spoof, put out by *The Onion*, but I figured, "It's working for her. Why mess with it?" In fact, after thinking it over, I decided to order my own copy for The Pie Shop bookshelves. It might be a nice read, and I'm sure my new apprentice Prentiss will get a kick out of it.

Prentiss, by the way, had already given me the link to this *Onion* video on the same topic: "Cosmopolitan Institute Completes Decades Long Study on How to Please Your Man."

If there's any one thing I've learned from The Morning Guy, I'd have to say that it's that "I have been doing it wrong" in general. And yet, I always hoped that meant that he had plenty of new stuff to teach me.

Apparently wrong. He's way too happy with a woman who not only anticipates his every need, such as sleeping in late this very morning, and she even has the ability to create—and satisfy—needs he never knew he had. Me, I would just have keep right on making him pie and asking for more golf tips. At least he still shows up to stock the soda machine. Sometimes.

So this brings to mind the Cosmo Quiz. I know you've taken at least one of them. We all have. How did you score? Did it help your relationship? Tell all.

By the way, what do *you* think I've been doing wrong?

As you know, the more often I fill out a personality profile, the more likely I am to be stunned by the results, so I'm not gonna do that no more. *You* can always tell me how I'm driving, how I'm baking, and how well you do or don't like my talent for karaoke.

After all, what are friends for?

When Clowns Play Golf

I was never one of these kids who are afraid of clowns. Apparently, that's one of those genes that skips a generation. If anything, some of my earliest, happiest memories are of being at the circus, watching clowns frolic around. I'm sure some of them were miming golf swings, and I'm pretty sure I've seen some of them in plainclothes here at The Slice of Heaven 24-Hour Pie Shop and Driving Range.

Yes, I've always liked clowns, even though my true circus love was the human cannonball, and I suppose I am still looking for someone like him. But can you imagine it? What would we talk about? Science, I guess. Alan Shepard. Lunar landers. Parabolas and projectiles. The distinct steak-like aroma of space. Heaven.

Ah, well. Perhaps that will happen some day. Meanwhile, I will be content to enjoy my growing friendship with The Clown whom I met at the Hollywood Halloween Party, along with Nurse Crotchett and The Morning Guy's delightful, but somewhat dull, Stepford Girlfriend. They are, all three, pretty good golfers, but The Clown is the best. After all, she has to play with giant crazy clubs that waffle around, and her spiked shoes are enormous. Surely her feet cannot be that big.

Some of the other players tend to go home early when The Clown is on the range. People get distracted by her honking and little dances, but I just love them. I actually like it that she doesn't speak, at least not in words, and that's refreshing after a day of pie shop chatter. For another thing, she is cheerful, but not unbearably cheerful like Steppie. No, The Clown has a confident glow about her, a delight in every little thing she encounters, whether it's an imaginary dog or a bucket of confetti.

The other night, The Clown came by with a golf cart full of her friends. I've known for some time that one of her primary interests in golf has been to drive the cart, but I don't for the life of me know where she got one, or how she was able to fit so many other clowns into it. Apparently, clowns do believe there's safety in numbers.

I could hear them coming down the road, from the direction of Pancho Villas, the radio tuned into the all-clown station: "Kathy's Clown," "Bozo Theme Song," "Send in the Clowns," "Bandy the Rodeo Clown," and other big-top hits.

I've got to say, once the a golf-cart load of clowns arrives at the driving range, pretty much every one else suddenly looks very well dressed, no matter what bizarre get ups they might have been wearing: Knickers, berets, argyle sweaters, and matching socks all look fine.

All those items are muy conservative compared to polka-dot pantaloons and gigantic bow ties. I noticed that lately The Clown has added a little Izod logo to her own lovely striped outfit, she now has a very nice new tam o' shanter on her head, and her golf bag matches her outfit.

By the same token, some of the super-sized drivers that I've see out here seemed tiny when placed next to the clubs that the clowns trot out. I've noticed, too, that the clowns seemed to have more trouble with lost balls than most golfers do.

I find this especially strange here at The Slice of Heaven 24-Hour Pie Shop and Driving Range, where it doesn't really matter where any one ball goes. Joe Sparkle Junior will find them all eventually when he makes his painfully slow sweep of the range with the E-Z cart picker.

The clowns also tended to scrutinize each ball very closely—sometime with magnifying glasses or randomly assembled jurors—before they'd place it on the tee, with grand exaggerated gestures. Sometimes they just juggle the balls and never hit any at all. Sometimes they hit joke balls that perform odd tricks such as boomeranging back toward The Pie Shop. I am not especially fond of that one.

I read recently about "Divot the Clown" who performs at golf events. I'm sure *my* clowns would never do that. I can tell that they hate to mix business and pleasure. They work hard at being clowns, and for them, golf is sheer pleasure, especially since they can play just outside of a pie shop.

Think about it: Clowns and pie? Yes, I do keep a lot of whipped cream on hand, just for them. You, on the other hand, may want to come by some other night if you see the clown-car golf cart parked out front.

Sweet Potato-Clock Pie!

Sue Ten never ceases to amaze me. Just tonight she brought me a plate of piping hot waffle fries, fresh from The Swing Barn's own organic Fry-O-Later.

She assures me that these delicious crispy potatoes are full of vitamin C, and she hardly even winced when I sprinkled malt vinegar over the plate and dug in. As it turns out, confectioner's sugar would have been just as good.

I tell you, the woman has a gift for potatoes. Granted, I do have an ongoing dispute with her about potatoes masquerading as pie crust, but I will never turn down her potato-sausage-cabbage casserole, her potato-brocolli-cheese soup, or her potato-bacon frittata. They are all perfect beyond question.

Just now, though, I've found out a little more about her love affair with The Spud. When her kids were in school, they all five, one after another, took on the daunting assignment of building a potato clock. I'm sure I remember seeing a kit for such a thing in the back of my brother's copy of *Boy's Life*, or *Grit*, or some such magazine, but I never attempted to assemble one of the things and had pretty much forgotten about the potato-as-battery concept.

Sue Ten never forgot, however, not after helping what must have seemed like a never-ending parade of frustrated middle-schoolers year after year re-create this particular piece of magic.

Never one to waste hard-gained knowledge though, Sue Ten continued to tinker with the damn things long after all five of the little Tens had long since grown up and moved away, leaving Sue and her husband Logan with time on their hands and several empty rooms.

I *could* take a minute now and fill you in on potato-clock technology just in case you are one of those rare individuals who doesn't know what a potato clock is.

Yes, you might be, although that would be surprising. Even your second-cousin Darnell knows what one is, and Joe Sparkle Junior has been running one in the E-Z Cart so he knows what time it is when he's out on the driving range picking up golf balls. I now have two in my turquoise conch cottage down at the end of the lane.

In fact, I did find a lengthy description on the "Hooting Yard" website, so I'm sure you can track down something similar. This particular treatise ended with one probing question: *"Which of us has not harnessed the power of the potato to control time?"*

Indeed. Heady stuff, I think, controlling time with potatoes. There's more to this particular story, though. I mentioned Sue's husband, Logan Ten, an affable guy with gifts of his own, a man who would go into any town and find a free buffet or a public reception in a matter of hours. He was a man who had mastered the art of the two-for-one, and usually came out with three.

Once Logan retired, though, he seemed content to collect his pension, and he began a peculiarly sedentary life of watching CNN 24-hours a day. During that time, though, Sue developed what can only be described as an obsession with potato-clock technology.

Her timepieces became ever more efficient, and her potato batteries reached impossible levels of duration. This, I understand now, accounts for the great variety of potato dishes coming out of The Swing Barn kitchen.

As Sue experimented with different strains of potatoes, she would buy spuds in quantity, and then cook up the leftovers after determining key factors such as longevity and quality of the best electrical charge.

While all that was going on, my mother and her sisters were running The Pie Shop, the driving range was but a fantasy, and I was on an extended walkabout, looking for an honest man, but settling for Pretty Boy Boyd instead. By the time I returned to South Florida, no one had seen Logan for quite some time, but Sue Ten was behind the bar at The Swing Barn, smiling and chatting as usual.

I was happy to see her, and we soon moved from small talk to more serious issues. "It must be hard on you," I said, "without Logan here now."

She looked puzzled. "What do you mean?"

"I'm sorry, Sue," I said. "I thought you and Logan had split up. No one has been him for so long."

"Oh, no," she said. "He's still here. He just doesn't go out anymore. You know how he always loved to watch CNN? Now he just does it 24 hours a day, but that's fine. His pension check is on automatic deposit."

That night, as I walked down to my turquoise cottage, I looked back at the Tens' double-wide behind The Swing Barn, and I noticed a certain glow coming from one of the bedroom windows. I knew Sue was still at The Swing Barn cleaning up, so I let my path diverge and headed north to see what was up.

Standing on my toes, I could peek into the window, and there I saw Logan, propped up in bed, smiling just as I remembered him, eyes closed though, and breathing softly. The glow was coming from the television set broadcasting CNN, as well as from an array of aromatherapy candles.

There was just enough light for me to notice that Logan had been outfitted with what appeared to be a couple of electrodes affixed to this temples. The main wires for the electrodes came from opening just above the bed's elaborate headboard featuring a reproduction of some of the murals in the "happy house" in the ancient city of Pompeii. A container of blue pills was nearby on the nightstand.

I moved silently to the next window and was stunned yet delighted to see shelf after shelf after shelf of potato batteries, some with clocks, some without, but all feeding into the network that was, apparently, keeping our dear Logan in his perpetually restful state.

"Yes," I thought, "Logan has his beloved news show on 24/7, the pension checks are being deposited, and Sue will never really be alone. No need to tell anyone about this at all."

I don't know what brought Sue and Logan to this juncture, but I do know she does seem as happy now as she ever was. As for Logan, he may even look a little bit more relaxed than before. Yes, I think he is doing fine.

Elbow Room

I've been spending most of my time in Pie Shop lately, not out on the range, due to a curious wankiness in my right elbow. Nurse Crotchett took a look at it and sent me off to physical therapy, which has meant driving into the village in real SoFLA traffic. It's definitely "the season" now, and I would be happier driving the E-Z Cart and picking up golf balls all day long.

Still, I'm of an age where I need to take care of these aches and pains, especially if I am to make it another 30 years to "The Singularity" and then live forever. I've already ordered Ray Kurzweil's new book on the topic for The Pie Shop bookshelves, and a number of us frequently like to discuss the ongoing ramifications of immortality, at least when we are not examining each other for rampant immorality, which we also enjoy discussing.

I'm surprised by how many people say they would not want to live forever, but Crotchett and I agree that we both have a lot to do and see, and 20 years may not be enough, even if we were wicked buff and trim, which we are not.

When my yoga guy, smoking outside the screen door while sipping a large cup of coffee, hears us take this tack, he yells in, "That's your ego speaking! There is nothing more. This is it. Be here now." We ignore him, so he takes another drag on his cigarette and walks over to the side of the building to supervise The Morning Guy's weekly ritual of detailing his BMW R 75/5s motorcycle.

In the greater scheme of things, I understand that my sore elbow is a mere bagatelle, a glimpse into sports medicine that I've found to be interesting, but nothing that I want to pursue through additional injuries, neither chronic nor episodic.

I do like the attention that I get during physical therapy, and I hope, in my own Pollyanna fashion, that this will ultimately improve my swing. I just have to convince my mind and body to accept new instructions about alignment and rotation. Yes, I am upbeat on this topic.

I am perpetually fascinated by the possibilities presented by the human body, both in space and on earth. Some days, I just can't wait to see what will happen next. For example, doctors have now performed the first successful full-face transplant. I thought that had been done long ago, but then I realized I was thinking of the John Travolta movie *Face/Off*.

I probably would not be going down this road at all, except for the fact that your second-cousin Darnell borrowed my car the other day to go over to the Pancho Villas gated community, and was too lazy to change the radio station. Consequently, he ended up listening to a lengthy discussion on bio-ethics, which left him feeling a little bit dazed and confused.

For most of us in The Pie Shop, though, the real face-transplant question was "Who would you like to look like, and why?" For me, the answer is easy: Julie Christie in *Doctor Zhivago*. Or maybe Elizabeth Taylor in *Cleopatra*. For Darnell, though, the idea of his body perhaps sloughing off his old face for a new one was too much too consider, and even Crotchett seemed to think that the ethics of wearing someone else's face bears additional discussion. She's in the right Pie Shop then.

I'd love to hear what you think about this. If money were no object, would you go for a new face? How about a new heart? New elbow? Let me know.

Zombie Golf

Can zombies play golf? Or should they?

I just finished reading *World War Z*, which is an impressive "oral history" of the zombie apocalypse. I say impressive because Max Brooks has done such a meticulous job of imagining and describing what aspects of life and civilization would be affected, and how, should the entire globe ever be infected by a zombie 'virus.'

I especially liked the concept that zombies are too dumb to open a door or crawl through a window, so a human bitten by a zombie in his or her car will most likely spend eternity in that very car, or at least until the car or the new zombie turns to dust. Note to vampire fans: Read some of Jemiah Jefferson's stuff if you really want a taste of the downside of immortality.

So, I've got to wonder, would a golfer bitten by a zombie live forever more on the links? If a being is not smart enough to open a door, can that creature still hit a ball? Or will it just follow its bloodlust over to The Swing Barn and wait for a drunk to roll out? What about a zombie bitten in a golf cart?

My world is pretty small these days, so I tend to take any little thing—like the zombie apocalypse—and try to apply it to my own life. I can pretty easily imagine Joe Sparkle Junior outrunning the zombie horde on the E-Z cart, but I'd worry about The Clown. She does tend to shuffle and she also does try to please, perhaps too much, and so does the Stepford Girlfriend. Yes, I'm afraid they'd be among the first to go. I'll miss The Clown, but Steppie really gets on my nerves.

I'm not really clear, either, on how long it takes for a new zombie to go from dead to re-animated. What if The Morning Guy were bitten while putting up Christmas decorations? Would he crash to the ground, wrapped in tinsel, and become the most festive zombie on earth? That's something to consider, too.

I was never a big zombie-fiction fan before reading this book, but now I find that there's a real void in The Pie Shop bookshelves. So remember us if you received some horrific story as a gift under your tree. We'll be glad to take it off your hands.

Meanwhile, I keep reminding myself that the undead can't open doors, but damn our doors are open much of the time. Twenty-four hours a day.

A New Year

The weather here for New Year's Eve in SoFLA was close to perfect, with clear skies and a waxing crescent moon. Sue Ten decided it was a good time to show another movie on the side of The Swing Barn and advertised *Casino Royale* accordingly.

A lot of us were happy to see that since we wanted to be prepared for the new James Bond flick *Quantum of Solace* which picks up exactly where the previous Daniel-Craig-as-James-Bond movie left off, but Sue surprised us by showing the Peter Sellers / Woody Allen version of *Casino Royale,* and that one ends in a wild night of cowboys on horseback, Indians with flaming arrows, Navy seals in scuba gear, and U.S. Marines, not unlike many regular nights at The Swing Barn.

The festivities at The Slice of Heaven 24-Hour Pie Shop and Driving Range were a little more restrained, and aimed at the non-drinking crowd. Prentiss, my pie-shop apprentice, did come up with a fabulous new corn-dog pie with an onion-ring crust, and she also served one of the possibilities in our search for "The Best Key Lime Pie Ever". Sadly, she garnished it with a slice of lime that was definitely not of the Key-lime variety, but more on that later.

Out on the driving range, we offered free balls from nine to midnight, and that always brings in a crowd. One new player was a guy with long gray hair and a handlebar moustache, who told me, "I was a caddy 50 years ago, and just now I am starting to play myself."

I told him that it's a game for optimists, since you can always believe that the next hit will be better. He said, "I was an optimist when I got here tonight, but I think I am a pessimist now." I hope he comes back. His accent smacked of New England, and I'm always a sucker for that.

As the evening progressed, I noticed several people from my physical therapist's office, but I think they were just trolling for business. Also, there were any number of Fem-Bots in short black dresses and high-high heels, trolling for business of another sort entirely. Granted, there aren't too many night spots out on the edge of the 'Glades where we live, and with the economy slumping as it is, we aren't in a position to turn anyone away.

Your second-cousin Darnell, by the way, did a great job of keeping the kids busy by having them create an "art car" which they covered with spray paint. I'm fairly sure my ex-husband Pretty Boy Boyd will like the new look of his formerly orange Toyota Celica.

He'll let us know when he gets back from New Orleans—if that *is*, in fact, where he really is. I hope so. He used to tell me that he had been a river boat gambler in a former life, and died in Louisiana. Perhaps history will repeat itself, not that I wish him ill. Of course not.

Nurse Crotchett brought along a truck load of fireworks, which she set about firing from the driving range, setting them off wherever she found an open slot. I tell you, it made for a great visual impact: golf balls flying into the air, fireworks lighting up the sky, the movie on the side of The Swing Barn, and the waxing crescent moon overhead.

I worried a little about some of the folks stumbling out of The Swing Barn into harm's way, but your second-cousin Darnell had the good sense to tether his goat Jonathan on a long line near the edge of the driving range, and for once, Jonathan earned his keep, and we resisted the urge to turn him into goat pie for yet another day.

I headed down to my turquoise conch cottage around 3:00 a.m., which was a nice change from my usual insomniac stroll to The Pie Shop at about that time, and fell into a few hours of troubling dreams.

One of the dreams, one I can still see pretty clearly, involved a wild car ride down a mountain road with Nurse Crotchett at my side and distressingly ineffective brakes. I probably don't need much help analyzing that one. I also dreamt that I had found an Asian baby, and gotten quite attached to it. The child grew to toddler size and was able to speak quite eloquently in no time, which is when she said, "I think I'm ready to go home now."

The final dream was that my orange hair color had gone strangely spotty, and was showing peculiar patches of mousy brown and gray. I can't understand that one at all. Tonight, the girls & I are dressing up to go to the ballet, leaving Darnell, Joe Sparkle Junior, and The Morning Guy in charge. I'm sure they will do just fine, don't you agree?

Key Lime Pie: The Search Begins

I was a little startled lately to read that "Key limes are the pink flamingos of Florida food, and they are a celebrated part of local color." I don't know what startled me more, the confusion of the color of the limes with pink or the realization that I have, apparently, missed the local Key Lime Festival again this year.

I presume that the author was referring to the rarity of both flamingos and Key limes, at least in Florida. There are flamingos in other parts of the world, and the same is true for "Key limes" which are actually from Malaysia.

How interesting, I think, that two items that say "Florida" to so many people are, in fact, phantoms from a not too distance past before plume hunters, hurricanes, and civilization tore through SoFLA.

Meanwhile, Prentiss and I are starting our search for the perfect Key lime pie. The challenge begins with some basic questions: Graham-cracker or pastry crust? Meringue or whipped cream? Cooked or uncooked filling? Fresh limes or lime juice? And, of course, can a Key lime pie be made with regular, old, every day, produce-department limes?

We'll let you know how our studies progress. I'm all for trying out a gingersnap crust, and I'm totally opposed to making the pie with any time of lime but a true "Key," but on the other hand, I'd rather use bottled juice from real Key limes than use fresh limes that aren't Key at all.

Prentiss and I do agree, however, with the no green food coloring rule, and we'll immediately rule out any recipe that even hints at artificial color.

I've been studying up a little on the history of the Key lime, and I'm not surprised to learn that no one knows who made the first Key lime pie. After all, who made the first apple pie, chocolate silk pie, or Alan Shepard pie. Oh, wait, that last one would be me.

It is possible, however, that the first Key lime pie of note was made by one "Aunt Sally," the cook for one William Curry, who laid the foundation of his fortune as a "ship salvager" in the mid-1800s. Today, the staff at the Curry Mansion Inn in Key West still crank out the pies. Perhaps a field trip is in order to investigate the current incarnation of Aunt Sally's pie.

There is, supposedly, no record of a Key lime pie recipe being penned before the 1930s. The supposition that "everyone just knew how to make the pie" puzzles me, because now I want to know how "everyone" forgot to make the pie. Was there a plague of amnesia, as there was in Gabriel Garcia Marquez's masterpiece *One Hundred Years of Solitude*? Was there perhaps a cataclysm of sorts, wiping out the knowing bakers? Or did the Key lime pie bakers decide en masse to take their knowledge with them to the grave? Or elsewhere? Like the Dry Tortugas maybe?

Here's another aspect of Key lime pie history. A crucial ingredient in Key lime pie is sweetened condensed milk, which was invented by Gail Borden in 1856. No sweetened condensed milk, no Key lime pie. At least nothing that resembled our current dessert. As for the limes, they probably started growing as soon as the Spanish explorers arrived in the 1500s, bringing yellow-green golf-ball size limes from Malaysia. And they continued to grow until the hurricane of 1926 which wiped them out. Most limes in Florida now are Persian, not Key.

The lime trees that remain are said to be "ferocious" in nature, and I'm not really sure what that means at all. Prentiss and I will try our hand at growing a few around the edge of the driving range, maybe start a little grove down the lane by my turquoise conch cottage.

Floridians are quite passionate about their Key limes, and their Key lime pie. In 1965, Florida State Representative Bernie Papy, Jr., introduced a bill that would have levied a $100 fine against anyone who advertised a Key lime pie not made with Key limes. Alas, the bill did not pass. But, in 1994, the legislature did decree Key lime pie as the Official State Pie.

Prentiss and I will be more than pleased to hear from you. Seriously, if you have a treasured Key lime pie recipe, we'll be glad to try it out, and we'll let know how all of us at The Slice of Heaven 24-Hour Pie Shop and Driving Range rate it. And you are always welcome to drop by and rate our Key lime pies, too.

Whole Earth Everything, Now on The Pie Shop Shelves

I'm excited to discover that the *Whole Earth Catalog*, including the *CoEvolution Quarterly*, is now available online. I can only hope that *Mad Magazine* will soon follow suit and provide me will full access to every single Alfred E. Issue. In truth, though, I would really rather have hard copy in my hands, and—in the case of *Mad*—a flashlight, too, so I can read it under the bedcovers after lights out.

While *Mad* helped grow the love of lyric poetry that Sue Ten and I still share, *CoEvolution* helped feed my lust for science, especially science that involves space exploration and the concept of other worlds, yet to be discovered. Okay, I'll admit that *StarTrek* did that, too, but *CoEvolution* made it seem legit.

I was living in the high desert of Arizona, far from my beloved 'Glades, when I was a truly avid reader of *CoEvolution*, and I often succumbed to the temptation to follow direct mail links, much as I now back link through blog posts. Of course, it was different in a small southwestern town, where the post mistress pretty much knew everything about me from reading my incoming postcards, not to mention the occasional incoming stamped and post-marked coconut.

So, I'm sure she was not at all surprised when my subscription to *CoEvolution* let to a membership in the L-5 Society, which in turn led to stranger and stranger letters of solicitation from people needing money to build their own space ships. I wonder how they made out. I would have donated more to the cause myself, but I really had enough trouble at the post office already.

I did just now do a quick search through the Whole Earth website index, and was disappointed not to find more positive reference to golf, or pie. I was sure they would at least mention the zen value of *The Inner Game of Golf*, and I was absolutely stunned not to find some whole-grain inedible pie recipes. Still, it was fun to revisit the space colony pages and imagine a future where we can all be together in a world of our own, where our priorities center around golf, pie, science, and poetry.

Oh, wait. We already have that, right here at The Slice of Heaven 24-Hour Pie Shop and Driving Range. All we need now is you.

Key Lime Pie Test (Rusty Pelican, Biscayne Bay, Florida)

I can't believe that I didn't take a picture of the pie before I ate it. I guess I'm just not fully committed to pie testing yet, but fortunately we are in the early days of the search and have barely begun to establish our testing parameters and matrices yet.

I will, therefore, need to return to The Rusty Pelican in Biscayne Bay in the very near future and sample another piece, preferably with Prentiss the Pie Apprentice in tow.

The Rusty Pelican is perhaps my favorite restaurant in the Greater Miami Area, one that Little Peach and I have visited several times, always with good results and always with a song in our hearts, the song being "Mustang Sally," but that's another story.

At any rate, I was happy to go there with a couple of friends who were only going to be in SoFLA overnight, and who were willing to brave the bitter cold to go out for the evening. I had imagined us sitting outside, looking across the bay at the city skyline twinkling in the night, but the 50-degree drizzle forced us inside, which was still a delightful experience.

I had had Key lime pie at the Rusty Pelican before, but years ago, before the search for the perfect slice began, so I had eaten it without the scrutiny it deserved. This time was different.

I thought the presentation was lovely, with the pale yellow filling garnished with a tart green glaze and a floret of whipped cream. Sadly, the slice of lime twisted on top of the whipped cream was of the Persian variety. Ah, well.

The graham cracker crust was innocuous as best, doing nothing to enhance or detract from the firm filling, which was thicker than many, and had a nice tang to it. The best feature of this pie was the super-tart glaze. The whipped cream was bland, but worked well with the glaze.

Over all score: B-plus

National Pie Day Eve

Here it is, the Eve of National Pie Day, and I find myself far from home, wondering how I ever managed to schedule this trip to the Northwest without factoring in the holiday. Ah, well. Prentiss has something planned, I'm sure. I just don't know what.

To add to my general disappointment in missing the annual festivities at The Slice of Heaven 24-Hour Pie Shop and Driving Range, I also discovered that people in the Northwest consider Key lime pie to be a "seasonal" dessert. Excuse me? It's not like they grow Key limes here and don't have any fresh ones right now. What can possibly be seasonal about Key lime pie? I am perplexed.

Of course, I ran into a similar situation years ago in Missouri when I went to the local Piggly Wiggly store to buy some salt pork for fish chowder, and was told that salt pork was "seasonal" and therefore unavailable. In that case, though, maybe salt pork is only harvested at certain times of year. Grim thought, and I shall not dwell on it.

Meanwhile, I am pretty sure that golf here is definitely seasonal, and not well played in the fog and/or ice, although I was pleased to see a woman on the ferry traveling with a driver and a putter. If she only had a wedge, she would be carrying all three of the most important clubs, as identified by both Harvey Penick and Ben Hogan.

I am fully enjoying Harvey Penick's *Little Red Book*, especially his comments on putting, which give me hope. For example, "Nothing is more important psychologically than knocking putts into the hole. Sinking putts makes your confidence soar, and it devastates your opponent."

I find I am enjoying putting more and more, and I'm looking forward to the day very soon when Joe Sparkle Junior and The Morning Guy finish the work on our new putting green. It's going a little slower than I would like since The Morning Guy has been distracted, both by football season and his Stepford Girlfriend.

Steppie, meanwhile, has been spending even more time here than usual as she has tried to find the right balance between cooing over her man, and giving him the space he needs to enjoy his football games and his pickled-eggs habit. She's putting her spare time to good use, though, working on her long game. It's been a treat to see her carefully lay out her golf balls and practice her swing. I believe she's been getting advice from the Fem-Bots, but I can't be positive on that. I do know she hasn't worn the same color-coordinated outfit twice in the past week.

I hope you all have a wonderful National Pie Day. I miss you like crazy, and can't wait to find out what all-you-all have been up to while I've been away.

I hope the SoFLA weather will be warm again soon, too. I understand it's been so cold there recently, that iguanas are falling out of trees. If our resident feral green iguana Hercules lands on someone, preferably my ex-husband Pretty Boy Boyd, the damage could be massive. We can only hope for the best.

A Couple More Slices of Key Lime Pie

All right, my dears, I did find Key lime pie in the Northwest, despite our initial stumbling block of the possibility that it might truly turn out to be a "seasonal" dish. Seriously: They've got a point. January is not a good time for the Washington State citrus crop.

Flyers was a fun place to meet and eat. I did enjoy the aeronautical theme, and general exuberance of the place. Or maybe that was just the exuberance of my dining companions? For dinner, I had a "prime rib dip" which I'd known in a former life as a "French dip," but I guess I should just be happy that they didn't call it a "Freedom dip."

I should never order this sandwich because I know it will never be as good as the one I had at the Limelight Cafe in Denver in 1972, but I am—as well you know by now—an optimist. Golf, after all, is a game for optimists, and so is the search for the perfect slice of Key lime pie.

Needless to say, the pie at Flyers met our expectations, which were low. We gave them points for presentation, and for adding nuts to the crumb crust, but the overall impression was that the whole concoction had only recently come out of the deep freeze. "Fresh" was not a word that sprang to mind, or to tongue.

The next day, we ventured by ferry to Port Townsend, and enjoyed some time out in the water. Granted, we were inside the ferry with our toes close to the heater, but we were there. I have a vague memory or two of being in Port Townsend before. Maybe you were there with me? I'm pretty sure Little Peach was my chaperone on at least one trip to that part of the world, and I did miss her this time around.

She has such a wonderful knack for asking all the right questions, and that's a gift that I envy. Traveling without her is always difficult, and when I get home, I know I will hardly be able to answer half of her well-placed questions, just because I didn't ask. Ah, well.

In Port Townsend, this time, I did have a marvelous piece of salmon for lunch, perfect in every way. I left a gold star on the posted menu on my way out the door. We did give this particular slice of pie high marks for the chocolate crust. Yes, indeed. I like a little experimentation, when the results pay off.

The filling, though, was exceedingly tart. We weren't surprised, though, since we had already leafed through the restaurant's cookbook, in fact we bought a copy, so we knew this particular offering was full of lime juice, no mention of fresh limes. At least they did not spoil the pretty presentation with a garnish of Persian lime, and I liked how the whipped cream was a decorative option.

I copied the recipe, which was pretty basic. Just speak up if you want to try it out yourself, and let me know what you think. It might be just the ticket to make you think of sunny SoFLA when you, too, are far from home.

String Theory Pie

Cooler weather, so
pie shop thoughts turn to squash
and spices
from all eleven dimensions
coexisting on the same
plane of faceted pyrex.

Will one fork ever be enough?

Will a fork be needed at all?

Spaghetti squash seems the
best choice for a filling that
never ends, especially if
you try to eat it
one yellow strand
at a time.

Looking for Golf in All the Wrong Places

I'm headed home from my long trip to the Northwest, and I really just can't wait to get back to SoFLA and find out what all-you-all at The Slice of Heaven 24-Hour Pie Shop and Driving Range have been up to in my absence. My apprentice Prentiss at least sent me a message today, just a few hours ago, in fact to tell me she misses me. I suspect she just now noticed that I've been gone for a week.

Sue Ten also called to say she'll be heading out of town shortly after I get back, so the changing of the guard will be quick and efficient. Neither Prentiss nor Sue Ten had much to report. I take this to mean that all is well, or they just really don't want me to worry about anything in advance. I haven't heard about any zombie attacks on SoFLA, so I will just hope for the best, and expect the worst, as usual.

In my week in Seattle and points north, I saw very little evidence of golf. There was that one woman on the Bainbridge Ferry, though. Then, in the SeaTac airport this morning, I saw an odd little sculpture of a golfer. I took a photo of the weird metal thing and sent it to The Morning Guy, but he did not seem to find it as amusing as I did.

I can tell he's already thinking ahead to long-term maintenance and is worried about me cluttering up the dooryard with such junk. If it were a little smaller, though, it might make a great hood ornament for the E-Z cart, or maybe it could ride on the roof. I'll have to take that up with Joe Sparkle Junior.

I've been passing some of my flight time paging through the *Sky Mall* book, which is my son Chandler's favorite magazine. His twin sister Rose prefers the parody version *Sky Maul*, and I have trouble telling the two books apart.

I'd hoped to find some nice golf gadgets in *Sky Mall*, but I am sadly disappointed. The one true golf item that I can find is a collection of 14 "club links" which are little monogrammed discs to be affixed to one's clubs. They are available in goldtone, silvertone, or black aluminum; no pink, no Palm Beach green. The message seems to be that these are for people in the habit of losing their clubs. I don't think I'll be encouraging this trend: If we help people identify their lost clubs, then we are only cutting down on our supply of rental and "try this" clubs.

I will, however, tell Sue Ten about the *Sky Mall*'s "Giant 8-inch Cupcake" which is supposedly easy to make, and fun to serve. You know as well as I do that she is always looking for something fun to serve, and yes she is still ready to serve. I'm hoping she'll be joining the FOAS (food on a stick) movement, soon, too. FOAS is not only fun to serve, but can be fun to eat, too, especially FFOAS (fried food on a stick) and DFFOAS (deep-fried food on a stick). Sue Ten is ready to serve, and I am ready to eat.

Too many days in the Northwest seem to have turned my head to thoughts of warmer clothing, even as I am mere hours from my flip-flops and shorts, so I've got to say I am fascinated by the *Sky Mall*'s "Carbon Fiber Heated Vest."

I'm not quite sure how this works, but I'm all for new technology and I've got to tell you that the phrase "laminated microfleece fabric" has the same distracting effect on me as seeing something shiny out of the corner of my eye. Yes, I want it, and I don't know why. I'm pretty sure it will improve my golf game on nights when the temps in SoFLA dip dangerously below 70. I need to be prepared.

Another tempting item in the catalog is the Kodak EasyShare Wireless Digital Frame, which promises, "The Power of the Internet, Now in Your Picture Frame." If I can have the Power of the Internet in a picture frame, why not in my golf bag, my pinkie ring, or even my rose tattoo? I'm intrigued. And, yes, Sky Mall does sell the "Swami Golf GPS" but I think they should combine GPS unit's "Insta-Lok" technology with their "Electronic Feng Shui Compass," and if they do that, I'll be happy to become the exclusive SoFLA distributor. Really, what could be better than GPS Feng Shui for golfers? Find out how far away the dragon is, align your shot accordingly, live well, and prosper.

Supposedly, the Feng Shui compass operates "with the same compass technology used in aerospace guidance systems," and that's not all! It also locates and calculates energy fields to help you align your physical surroundings. I can't wait to get one of those for the driving range. We may have to move a few palm trees around, and reroute our feral green iguana Hercules on his daily stroll, but I'm sure this will all pay off in better golf for all of us, with or without the Swami GPS Golf option.

All right, my dears. We are just about to land, and you know I'll soon be out on the range under the lights, so come on by. I've got hours to go before I sleep.

Intergalactic Sports

Sorry to be so tardy in getting this news to you, but the possibility of more of us playing golf in space may be a reality before we know it. I just read that a former NFL linebacker is hard at work training future space tourists to get in shape to have serious fun in zero gravity.

By the way, it's not too late for you to contribute to my own zero-gravity fund so I can be the first person to eat pie in space. I'm still only about $5,000 short of what I need for my practice run.

This guy, though, may be on to something by taking his "space sportilization" program to Abu Dhabi where people may well have a tad more disposable income than they do right now in SoFLA.

What's really amazing to me, though, is how he manages to make this concept seem downright boring, if his YouTube video about the project is the best that he can do.

I'm pretty sure that almost anyone at The Slice of Heaven 24-Hour Pie Shop and Driving Range could show more enthusiasm for playing almost any sport in space than he does, but what do I know?

And yet we wonder why American kids are falling short in science. I say, let them eat pie. In space.

Go Cry on Somebody Else's Shoulder

The warmer weather here in SoFLA and the full moon have certainly combined to bring out the people. Just a week ago, the silence was fairly staggering, but tonight we've had a full house since the moon came up, and not much sign of a slow-down yet. I'm sitting outside The Pie Shop, just watching the balls arc up into the air, and listening to the washer spit out bucket after bucket after bucket. Life is good.

For some reason, while I was practicing my swing earlier, I kept hearing Frank Zappa's song, "Go Cry on Somebody Else's Shoulder". I don't know why. Perhaps it's just a Zappa carryover from a conversation with a friend who shared the news that he wished he'd been named Moon Unit. Knowing his father, though, I'm a little surprised that he wasn't named Moon Unit.

After that song faded away, it was replaced by Bonnie Raitt's "You Gotta Know How," which is always a good soundtrack for homemade video greeting cards. At least I think so. I'll have to add both of those to The Pie Shop juke box. We haven't had any new tunes for a while, and we are overdue.

Funny, but with such a crowd out tonight, I found that I talked less, concentrated more, and let quite a few thoughts roll around my head. Sue Ten has been away for a while, but called in on video to let me know she's alive and well. She always asks what great Zen thoughts I'm having, and I often think I should be writing them down on the back of my hand so I don't forget when she asks.

Yes, I do have great thoughts, but then I get hungry, and a large chocolate shake usually chases them away.

Tonight, though, I made a serious effort to try to hold on to a few, and I was doing pretty well until your second-cousin Darnell came by and distracted me completely with the news that he had just finished reading *A Beautiful Mind*, the biography of mathematician John Nash.

"It was much more interesting than the movie," he said. "In the movie, I got the idea that John Nash was a pretty smart guy, and he saw things that weren't there, but who doesn't do that?" I waited for more. "In the book though, I really couldn't understand what he was doing most of the time, so I figure he has to be a whole lot smarter than anyone I know, even you." Again I waited.

Darnell went on. "Another thing that I didn't get from the movie was how sad it was for him not to be crazy any more, how sad it must have been for him to give up all the magical stuff that was going on when he was nuts. I don't know. I just think it must have been sad, just like the way Boyd acts when he's sober."

Darnell, of course, was referring to my ex-husband Pretty Boy Boyd, and I'll say Darnell made a good point there. I, personally, got so I couldn't stand Pretty Boy's alcoholic flights of fancy, but he certainly was never alone when he was drunk. He always had his selfs (himselfs?) to talk to, and he was certainly a legend in his own mind.

With John Nash, and Pretty Boy, too, the difference between perceived reality and "normal" reality seems fairly clear to observers, but who are we kidding? Most of us are on the inside looking out, deciding how we want to present ourselves to the world, but a few of us have that decision already made for us in advance.

Me, I live in a world of pie and insomnia where clowns drop by to play golf, your second-cousin Darnell lives with a goat, and my best friend keeps her semi-comatose husband alive by hooking him up to potato-powered batteries. I'm certainly not in any position to argue about reality with anyone.

Sometimes, too, I think maybe there's an alternative universe in which The Morning Guy has come to his senses and is not vacationing in Key West with his Stepford Girlfriend. Yes, I'm sure there's a place where he and I are living happily ever after. But if that's true, there's probably also an alternate universe in which he's carried off by a pack of Fem-Bots, and I never see him again.

That makes me sad, too, and what can I do but . . . go cry on somebody else's shoulder?

The Gimme

I was born knowing how to make pie, but golf is always brand new to me. Learning to bake pie is a sweet succession of improvements: lighter, flakier, zingier; but golf still surprises me. Both are nice ways to spend time; one is a steady and comfortable satisfaction, while the other is an unexpected burst of delight.

The latest burst has been my discovery of the golfing term "gimme." I tell you, it just cracks me up. I first read about it in my copy of Harvey Penick's *Little Red Book*, in which he advises parents against giving their golfing children gimmes. "Hole every putt," said Penick, "no gimmes." Tough love or real world? Maybe both.

I like it. Keep playing until you see that ball drop into the hole. Make no assumptions about what that little sucker is going to do on its own.

I read some time ago about a championship bowler who was asked in an interview: "What was bowling like for you as a kid? How did it feel back then when you missed the pins?" The pro replied, "I never missed the pins. I don't know what that feels like."

Now, come on. All kids miss the pins. Gutter balls are a sad but true part of kiddie bowling. As the interview went on, though, the bowler explained that his father owned the bowling alley, back in the days of pin boys. The pin boys were instructed to set up the pins just a few feet from the foul line. As the boy grew older and played better, the pin boys set the pins farther and farther down the alley—but not unless they knew he could hit them.

In some ways that's a gimme, too, but I see it more like making sure the ball always goes in the hole. I wish I had learned to bowl that way, under the guidance of someone who truly wanted me to know success.

Of course, the next question is, if I had had that experience, "Would I still be me?"

Sometimes people ask me for pie recipes. Then, after they read the recipe, they follow-up with suggestions and recommendations for changing it. I usually say, "That's fine. Do what you want, but don't call it my recipe anymore."

In truth, I feel the same way about making changes in me. I can change. Sure, I know I can. Probably. I might even learn to be more like the Stepford Girlfriend, become more of a perky chameleon, but I have to wonder what I might lose along the way. Would I still be me?

Then again, who else would I be? I suppose I'm committed to the concept of holing every putt, but damn I do like that gimme idea, too. Life could be so easy, if I could just change my definition of me.

You may wonder why I'm so philosophical right now. Don't worry. It will pass. It always does.

Steampunk Cafe

Sue Ten will be going on vacation soon, and that means I will be responsible for keeping the potato batteries in her bedroom running so her husband Logan's semi-comatose brain will get just the right dose to keep his heart beating and his mind tracking The Weather Channel and CNN.

Outside of that, Logan is pretty much an "easy keeper," which is what my ex-husband Patrick-the-Liar used to call me, endearingly, of course, and I wasn't even in a semi-coma, although after a few years with Patrick, it was increasingly hard to tell. I suspect that I sleepwalked through much of that part of my life. Now, I just go with the flow of rampant insomnia, and don't worry about it.

It's easy enough to leave my turquoise conch cottage and head up the lane to The Pie Shop where I can hit a few golf balls, have a plate of pie, check the Post-It notes covering my computer, read a little poetry, and try not to let it all mesh together too much.

I suppose I could ask your second-cousin Darnell to help out with Logan, but I need him at The Pie Shop to help me with some re-decorating. After looking at an antique golf periscope, I've been thinking that maybe The Pie Shop needs more of a steampunk flair.

If you don't know what steampunk is, just let your thoughts drift to an illustrated copy of any Jules Verne book, or just picture Captain Nemo at home in the salon of the Nautilus. It's the future, visiting us from the past, with all the elegance it can muster.

Take, for example, the idea of a steampunk computer. I want it, Now imagine a steampunk jukebox, coffee maker, kitchen, cash register, radio, golf-ball washer, neon lights, soda machine, dishwasher, lawn mower, golf cart, and more.

I've never thought of myself as a Luddite, but maybe that tendency has always been lurking there. I remember watching TV with the twins when they were in junior high, and we'd often see a public service announcement aimed at kids and asking, "What can you do to change the world?"

Chandler and Rose would say in unison, "We'd go to central control and smash all the machines!" Yes, that would certainly change the world, but where did they get such an idea?

No, I'm not really against technology. In fact, after a week of living out on the other side of the edge of the 'Glades, I have new appreciation for all the magic in the air that keeps me in constant touch with you, and really, I don't know what I would do without you right over there, telling me what I need to do to keep on keeping on. I appreciate it, and I thank you in my heart every day.

Then again, I do think technology could be ever so much more elegant than it is most of the time, so I am pledging to do what I can to re-create The Slice of Heaven 24-Hour Pie Shop and Driving Range as a steampunk Mecca.

At least, that's my idea today, but if I ever get in a good night's sleep, who knows what I may think up next? Maybe a steampunk potato battery? I'm sure Logan won't mind if I do a little experimenting on his power supply while Sue is on the road, at least not as long as his Social Security checks keep rolling in.

Get a Grip

We have a wonderful collection of left-behind golf clubs here at The Slice of Heaven 24-hour Pie Shop and Driving Range. Seriously, they are all sizes, shapes, lengths, and shafts. Sometimes they are bent beyond recognition, but more often they are just abandoned. Actually, that only seems fair, once you take into consideration how often clubs—especially putters—desert their owners.

Even Camilo "Spiderman" Villegas has been photographed tossing a putter away, or at least giving up when it obviously has decided to take off in search of its own fortune, with no thought at all about the outcome for poor Camilo. Then again, other golfers claim to have stayed with hot putters, right to the astounding end.

Putters, more than any other clubs, tend to operate independently of their owners, and as soon as we are able to open our putting green, I imagine our "lost and found" bin will be overflowing with runaway putters.

Until then, we'll work with what we have. The Morning Guy has recently added re-gripping to his list of useful talents. Now that football season is over, he has a little more time on his hands, and I think he kind of likes the smell of the adhesive. Of course, his Stepford Girlfriend will say she likes it, just as long as she thinks he really does like it.

Re-gripping is quiet work, which The Morning Guy enjoys, and I absolutely love seeing the old clubs come sparkling to life once again. So much of golf is truly organic and tactile, it truly isn't very hard at all to believe that putters can, in fact, fly away, and no one really knows where they go, or why.

We'll make a deal with you, too: If you think your putter is about to go on the lam, snatch it up and bring it on in here. We'll be happy to make a trade with you, and we'll throw in a free piece of Key Lime Pie, too.

This week, by the way, we're trying out the variation with meringue and a pastry crust. I think you'll like it. Come on by and let me know.

An Urgency of Pay Phones

A few days ago, I was driving south on U.S. 1 in SoFLA when I spotted a run-down convenience store, windows obscured with hand-lettered signs in Spanish, and the sight triggered a memory of a day when I had stopped at that very place to call my second ex-husband Pretty Boy Boyd to draw a bead on his level of sobriety before continuing home.

I don't remember the conversation, but I'm pretty sure it was an emotional one, as so many of our pay-phone calls tended to be. In fact, I now believe that the correct term for a group of pay phones should be "urgency." Yes, an urgency of pay phones. When dormant and unused, as they typically are today, they seem so benign, but did you ever really need to find one? Did you ever scramble for change on the floor of the pick-up truck and focus all your homing instincts on a pay phone?

The first one would be out of order, and the second one would be unavailable, its attention fully given over to that enormous woman you always saw at Wal-Mart, wearing a flower-strewn sundress on the first day of spring. Finally, you pull up to one, run to the phone with the truck engine still growling, and make the call. Yes, urgency.

At least at an outside phone, you might talk in a low voice, barely above a whisper. Now, the cell-phone generation shares everything with the immediate neighborhood, but those conversations are simply not that interesting to me: "Guess where I am?" or "What kind of milk did you want?" or "What do you mean it's my turn to drive the carpool?" Mundane, at best.

24-Hour Pie Shop and Driving Range

Overheard pay phone conversations tend to be better stories, and I love a good story. (Otherwise, I probably never would have gotten married, but I wanted to continue to follow the narrative thread.)

For example, early one morning, walking by the Walgreen's in South Beach before dawn, I saw a tall, dark-haired, mini-skirted woman leaning desperately into the pay phone receiver: "You don't understand," she was saying, "they made the buildings too tall in Miami. You really don't understand. All the buildings are sinking! Listen to me!"

I've always wished I had loitered there longer to hear more, and I can still feel the story calling to me. What if I had stayed and offered my help? Where would I be now?

Yes, an urgency, compounded by knowing that once she hung up, the contact would be lost. She had to know she had one chance to make her point. If she called again, the person on the other end might not answer, and there are no call-backs on pay phones today.

There was a time, though, when pay phones were more aggressive than they are now. They would ring out at random intervals, beckoning passers-by to answer. "Sylvia?" the voice would say. "Sylvia? Are you there?" She wasn't. Or maybe you would be the one hunkered down nearby, waiting for the call, growling at anyone else, saying, "Hey! Don't be long! I'm expecting a call." Bloody fist fights have broken out over less.

Picture a cell phone on a table. Doesn't do much for you emotionally, does it? Now picture a pay phone, the receiver dangling, a soft voice calling out, "Hello? Hello? Dave?" Imagine a reporter calling in a story on a cell phone. Nope. Doesn't happen. Blog it in on the smart phone. Now drop back to the guy in the fedora sitting in the glass-and-wood booth: "Hello, city desk? Give me rewrite!" (I always wanted to do that.)

Where would Superman and Dr. Who be without phone booths?

Then again, from the other end of the line, snuggled up comfortably at home, you might have to struggle to make out the spoken words against the backdrop of jukebox and bar noise: "I need you to come get me right now" or "Don't hold supper for me" or "Jimmy says ger flog and we mast up to la overture."

No, I don't miss receiving those calls at all, but I will confess to having made maybe one or two. I probably still owe your second-cousin Darnell an apology for that night I called from a truck stop in Kansas and woke him up at 2:00 a.m. for reasons that now escape us both.

So why do I want a pay phone at The Pie Shop? Perhaps this is part of my move toward the steampunk lifestyle, or maybe I'm just nosey and want to overhear better stories.

I'm thinking maybe an old style black one, with a rotary dial, inside by the front door, within easy earshot of the cash register.

I promise I'll always give you change if you need it, and I'll even keep a pencil on a string and a pad of paper near by. From time-to-time, I'll leave a some dimes & nickels in the coin return for the kids to claim.

Out by the road, though, I want a real phone booth, under the solitary street lamp.

When we are basking in the warm glow of the pie-shop lights, inhaling the warm scent of apples and cinnamon, we can look out there and remember all the pay phone calls of our old solitary lives, and remind ourselves how lucky we are to have each other, face-to-face, right here, right now.

And maybe on the jukebox, we'll listen to Hal Ketchum singing "The Coast is Clear," or perhaps Joan Baez singing "Diamonds and Rust": *Where are you calling from? A booth in the midwest.*

That line still tugs at my heart. What about you? What's your pay-phone story? Have a seat at the counter, and tell me all about it.

Remember, at The Slice of Heaven Pie Shop and Driving Range, we're here for you, 24 hours a day.

Spring Training

Despite the absence of Sue Ten, I did manage to slip away on Saturday and go to a Red Sox spring training game against the Baltimore Orioles.

My standing-room-only ticket provided me with a nice spot right at the fence, and I had the good fortune to have excellent fans on either side of me. To my right, there was a seven-year-old girl, dressed all in pink, including pink Red Sox hat, the accessory of my dreams. I do wish I would just go buy one for myself, but then what would you get me for my birthday?

She also had a pink camera, and was busy snapping shots through the fence. Her dad told me they had been to Fenway last fall, and she got to run the bases. What a treat.

To my left, a couple from Miami stood enjoying their hot dogs. We soon got into a conversation about Cuba, and found out that all three of us had been there at different times.

By the end of the afternoon, we had bonded over tales of growing up in New England—the husband and I had lived about 10 miles apart, but went to different schools in different states, and never knew each other despite graduating from high school the same year—and during the conversation, the question came up, "Were you always a baseball fan?"

For me, the answer was no. In my neighborhood, as I may have mentioned before, girls played outfield for both teams, way outfield, and I am talking about a real field. Some times we were so far out field we could not even see who was at bat.

My folks did not watch sports, not that I can remember, but my grandmother was an avid Red Sox fan, and we kids were not allowed to talk to her when a game was on. She had some kind of jury-rigged gadget that would let her turn the sound off during commercials, so we could talk then. Commercial over, sound on, talk over.

Still, I did always like the idea of baseball, the mathematics of it mostly I think. The sound, the look, the smell. I'm still not a huge fan of baseball on television, but I will be listening in on MLB radio once the real season progresses.

After I met Pretty Boy, baseball came back into my life. I had managed to ignore most sports during previous relationships, but the reality that I was dating a New York Yankees fan had an odd impact on me. Some sort of primordial energy bubbled up inside me, and I understood that I had to arm myself against the Spawn of Satan. My Red-Sox imprinted genetic code won out, and now I know what it means to take a stand.

Perhaps that is a small thing to you, but to a crowd-pleaser like me, that's a major step in personal empowerment and self-definition. I discovered that I really enjoy the emotion of baseball. I get a huge kick out of tee-shirts that say, "I root for two teams: The Red Sox and whoever beats the Yankees."

Had I but world enough and time, I'd go to a stadium ball game every day, just to revel in the pleasure of being there, worries set aside, high-fat food in hand, sun in my eyes, and lucky socks on my feet. I rarely remember any of the plays or the players, except the same few that you already know, so the live games are also an "in the now" experience for me.

Spring training games are usually fairly free of broadcast press-box chatter, and I like that, too. There are always other fans to tell me what's going on, and to share their stories. Sun Ten and I even went to see the Italian team play the Marlins. That game, in an almost empty stadium, was as much a thrill as any game I've ever attended. Sue cheered and chortled. We saw Elvis selling popcorn, and we saw a guy wearing a marlin hat. No, not a "Marlins" hat. A fish, on his head. Then we laughed all the way home.

I'm sure she doesn't mind that I left The Pie Shop and The Swing Barn in the hands of The Pie Apprentice, your second-cousin Darnell, and The Morning Guy, for the afternoon. After all, it's March in SoFLA, and what could be better than that?

On the Other Side of the Edge of the 'Glades

I've been back from my trip to the other side of the 'Glades for more than a month, and I'm still waking up wondering where everyone is. I've had some remarkable dreams since returning to my own king-sized pillow-top bed, too, dreams in which my team-mates and I were Navy seals, or old-time sailors, or just obsessed campers, traveling in our pod of sea kayaks through the tangled green mangrove islands in and out of sunsets and star-filled skies.

Even now, though, I am surprised by how tired I am. This goes beyond my normal insomniac want-to-take-a-nap mode. This is bone tired. I focused on this trip for months, using it as my reason for pushing up my exercise limits, not just at the driving range, but in yoga class and biking, and out and about with Sue Ten and our rag-tag walking group. I even made a point of getting to the pool in the Village for swim training with a triathlon coach. Now all I can do is sit quietly and read *Wind in the Willows* on my iPod Touch, which as you know I have ensconced in a hollowed-out purple-leatherbound book.

Driving back from the trip, I remember thinking how happy I was that I would be home by 2:00 or 3:00 with plenty of time to go to the pool for a swim. I was convinced that I could knock at least five stokes off my swim, I felt so buff; and, of course, I'd be able to add unknown yardage at the driving range. Then I hit Alligator Alley heading east, and the warm sun began to lull me. It wasn't long before I pulled into a rest area and closed my eyes, waking up 20 minutes later in a whole new frame of mind.

The Slice of Heaven

By the time I made it to my turquoise conch cottage, all I wanted to do was sleep. I nodded to Hercules, our resident feral green iguana who was busily eating the hibiscus bush near my porch, walked in the door, and that was that. I woke up again around 3:00 a.m. to the sound of golf balls out on the all-night range, and I smiled to be home again.

During the next day or two, I enjoyed sharing stories of the trip with some of the folks at The Pie Shop. I told them about scorpion-eating women, traveling by starlight, visiting graves of long-ago settlers, gliding through the water. I told them, too, that my favorite part was the "solo," the day and night when I camped alone, as did the entire team. I made a sundial out of stones and shells and wrote a poem for Little Peach. I counted my blessings, which was easy. I took a lot of photos. I ate an apple and an orange and some trail mix. And, I watched the sun go down and saw the flash of green, to my everlasting delight.

On solo, I fell asleep in my little shelter, made with a tarp and an old sheet that Little Peach left at my house for a drop cloth. It had always seemed too bad to get paint on the cute little koala bears all over it, so I'd stuffed it into the back of my closet, and pulled it out for the trip. I loved looking up at those little koalas; they made me feel connected to my "real" world, the one that seemed so distant from the mangroves and the sea kayaks.

I carried most of you with me during the trip, imagined you stirring up the pot of beans for supper, or plotting out our course. I thought about what you might have added to our conversations, and how sweet it would have been to have breakfast together on one of those isolated beaches. I discovered that my yoga practice really paid off when it came to getting dressed standing on one leg, outside in primitive conditions: Balance, my dear Grasshopper, balance.

Did I change? Did I grow? Did I discover any new Zen thoughts? Did I improve my golf swing? Did I find any new recipes? Yes, absolutely. I came home in a state of harmony and oneness, content. I had accepted a challenge and felt that I met it. I felt strong and healthy and on course in my life, the life I share with all of you at The Slice of Heaven 24-Hour Pie Shop and Driving Range.

I doubt that I could have made the trip, or enjoyed it, without you in my heart and mind. In the past year or so, since I got myself single, I've learned what it is to have friends like you in my life; people who do not hesitate to shake me up when I need it, or call my bluffs (of which there are many), or tell me when I am drifting dangerously near the plummeting falls. I love seeing in you in what my new team-mates saw in me.

And once again, I discovered that my life in SoFLA has been a series of breathing lessons.

Sundial for Little Peach

In a house full of clocks
she lives on sundial time:
I know that well, and so,
alone on a beach with
sunlight to spare, I gather shells
and make for Peach a
sundial clock that she
will never see but always
understand as the passage
of the sun through the
beach's decay reminds us
daily that shells are not stone
and even the most
vibrant coral fades from living
being to silent debris
just as we move in our own orbits
a degree at a time.

Linton and Swinton and Michigan

In just a few days, Sue Ten will be home from her tour of the unknown universe, so I am scrambling to remember whatever it was that I promised to do in her absence. I did check in on her semi-comatose husband Logan every day, making sure that he was receiving just enough electrical charge from the room full of potato-clock batteries to keep a heartbeat going, and a social security check coming.

I upgraded a few of the spuds that seemed to be going a little black and shady. I wonder if yams would work as well, or if they would just turn his dreams to orange? I don't know.

By the way, right before Sue left on her trip, she'd been cast in a leading role of our local Little Theatre's production of "Linton and Swinton and Michigan" an inspiring story of taking a wilderness and somehow turning it into a Village by the Sea. I just can't seem to get the soundtrack out of my mind, can you?

Maybe the reason I can't get it out of my mind is because The Little Theatre has been rehearsing almost non-stop over at The Swing Barn, and it's been that kind of SoFLA perfect weather where we do actually throw open our windows and doors.

I love this story of the hearty pioneers from Michigan heading to the Atlantic coastline to tame the swamp and rusticate on the miles of beach. Just to the north of us, Mr. Flagler led the way, and he set the bar high. I love going to Palm Beach and visiting the mansion he built for his third wife, soon after coming to the realization that Wife Number Two was doubtless insane and would be much better off in an asylum. Yes, he must have been a rare and compassionate man to understand mental health so well. Wife Number Two was spared the stress of her husband's private-train-car lifestyle, and The Mistress got a nice promotion. Everyone won.

But back to our musical. Let me tell you, the stage decor is quite impressive, and I think Sue will be ready to step right into her role as Vivienne Venitianne, the pineapple heiress who wins the heart of the Villagers with her mighty wit and repartee.

And they, in turn, are there for her after the pineapple blight and the vagaries of the market force her to give up the high life and find true contentment as a Red-Cross certified lifeguard.

Now you may wonder how a musical comedy can be in production without its star, but that's not really so hard to understand. The character Vivienne suffers from a peculiar inability to sing. She just plain freezes up, but not until she gets in a truly painful line or two, much to the general merriment of all, advancing the plot scene by scene as she does.

Perhaps coincidence, but Sue Ten won't have to act out that part. She's long been active in her work to celebrate the tone-deaf and the non-musical, and those of us who sing for joy, not for pleasure, are ever grateful for her openness to our afflictions.

This could be why we never get much of a crowd at The Swing Barn on Karaoke night, but shouldn't every one have a chance? I have already mentioned the motif: "Introverts with Microphones (A Dangerous Combination)". But that's another story.

My big surprise for Sue Ten is this: While she has been away, I've arranged through Prentiss to hire a crew of budding young filmmakers to film a documentary about the making of "Linton and Swinton and Michigan."

They will be at the Tri-Rail Station on Thursday night, waiting to greet her with klieg lights shining. Granted, she will have been traveling for about 27 hours non-stop by then, but we want her to know we are on the scene, and we want her to know we care.

I may even make a pie.

Swing Thoughts Poem

I've been reading a lot lately about "swing thoughts" and how to get your mind right each time you lift a club to send a ball to a predetermined target. Usually I just think about you.

Swing No Thought

So much advice, so little time.
"Keep your head down."
"Straighten that elbow."
"Open your hips, but not too early."
"Let the club do the work."
"Breathe!"
"Keep your eye on the ball."
"Let your legs do the work."
"Consider the target, not the ball."
The list of thoughts will wear you out. How
> to stand
> to swing
> to breathe
> to feel
> to think
> to move
> to count
> to watch
> to see
> to imagine
> to play.

If only one thought could get you there
> from tee to target,
> how delicious that would be
> like a slice of cold apple crisp
> with your first cup of coffee,
> like a sliver of pastry
> promising more.

If only one thought could cover it all:
> trajectory
> velocity
> momentum
> distance
> the past
> the present
> the future
> the sound of the wind
> the gossip
> the grass.

Did you choose the right club?
Did you lock the car?

24-Hour Pie Shop and Driving Range

Was tonight someone's birthday?
Did that guy flip me off?
If only one thought could
open your mind
show you success,
just seconds away,
a beckoning future
in which you've controlled
    trajectory
    velocity
    momentum
    distance
    the past
    the present
    the future
    the sound of the wind
    the gossip
    the grass.
Unlikely, I think
so maybe instead
simply revel
in rhythm and tempo.

Maybe instead
marvel to see
the ball in fierce flight—
or skipping,
like a stone,

in search of a river.

Laugh.

Things happen for
a reason.

Things happen for
no reason at all.

Enjoy the possibilities.

Lift the club,
Breathe in and smile.
You're good to go.
You'll either be right or wrong.
In either case,
You'll learn something new.

Don't think of the outcome.
Don't think at all.
And when you are done,
Let me know how that works.
Yes,
Quiet your mind.

Step up to the future, and
look for me there.

National Pie Championships (Part Two)

I am excited beyond belief to be accepted as a judge at the National Pie Championships this month, even though it does mean leaving my beloved SoFLA once again for the Northern Realm somewhere near Orlando. (Golf friends, please take note that this event is the equivalent of The Masters, or The U.S. Open. Yes, it's The Big Time.)

I'm hoping that Nurse Crotchett, Little Peach, or one of the other regulars can join me for the event, but I'm sure I'll be fine on my own, happy in my work and fully enjoying the Never-Ending Pie Buffet.

When I called Little Peach to say that I was going to be a judge at the National Pie Championships, she laughed for a very long time, and then she said, "Have you told the kids?" I said I had emailed them, and she said, "They are probably laughing too hard to reply."

Now why would she react that way? I certainly would be happy for her if she had been selected to judge an Orchid Championship or a Model Train Championship. Sometimes I think she does not fully appreciate my dedication to pastry, or my dedication to golf for that matter.

A couple of days later, though, she called back and left a fairly lengthy message on my answering machine. Here is a reasonably accurate transcription of what she had to say, having had some time to reflect upon the fullness of my accomplishment:

"Okay," she said, "I'm thinking I'm about this on a long drive back from Dade City, and I'm thinking about this to myself. Okay. You have to be judging pie, hopefully Key lime pie, and my big question is: What does one wear as a judge in a pie-judging contest? Do you have to have a special apron? Do they give you a wooden spoon? Do you do have to wear something with 'Betty Crocker' written across it?

"I mean, did you have to whip up a little something? I don't know. I was kinda wondering. Is there a special judge bow that you have to wear? I don't know. What does one wear to judge pies? So anyway, then I thought, 'Heels!' What about your gold heels?

"Those would be perfect, with a nice little apron and a fresh green wooden spoon, with a green gingham bow tied on the end of the spoon? What do you think? I'm getting a picture here. Oh! What about a tiara? Something with 'BC' for Betty Crocker or 'J' for Judge. Maybe you could push a button and it could light up? I don't know, but now I've got all these visuals. Talk to you later. Bye."

Just right off hand, she might be right about my gold heels, but I still don't think she is taking this very seriously.

I am, though, and I've got just a few days to do my homework and really learn the criteria of pie judging. Just as a tease, though, I'll tell you two traits that I will be reviewing: One is "mouthfeel" and the other is "memorableness."

Oh, yes. It's the Big Time for me, now.

You Got to Have Friends

The other night, Sue Ten reached deep into her rucksack of old movies and came out with *Sheila Levine is Dead and Living in New York City* to show on the side of The Swing Barn, while those of us who were so inclined relaxed in our portable lounge chairs, sipping our beverages of choice. I brought over a cooler full of "Key Lime Pie on a Stick," or at least full of Prentiss's latest attempt to perfect that treat. She is getting close, but we see no need to tell her that.

The best thing about the movie *Sheila Levine* is the soundtrack, specifically Bette Midler singing "Friends." Even before movie night, I've had that song in my head, and you know how I love to share that sort of idiosyncrasy with you. That song came out when I was younger than my kids are now, so young that I didn't even know I had insomnia because I was up all night anyway. It seems to me that friendship comes easier in youth than it does in those middle years when focus for so many of us, especially women, narrows down. Now though, I feel the scope widening again, and as I saw you chatting and enjoying the movie, I couldn't help but count my blessings.

We try to make sure that The Slice of Heaven 24-Hour Pie Shop and Driving Range is a place where all-you-all can leave your troubles behind. By that, I don't mean leave them here. We can't use them. We are not saying "pack up your sorrows and give them all to me" because that's just plain crazy. We're saying this is a place where you should be able to walk in the door and instantly forget all about that horrible dream you had last night that erupted into a full-body spasm.

We are not always successful at creating that level of therapeutic ambiance, but that's our goal. While I'm happy to dispense hugs, both free ones and the premium two-dollar kind, to the ones I love, I'm also on the lookout for toxic people so I can ward them off. Who knows? They may be the first wave of the coming zombie apocalypse, and we can't encourage that. Zombies are messy golfers, and I am not ever going to put brain-pie on the menu. They simply don't belong here. They are the ultimate in toxic people.

I recently read a nice test for judging toxicity in people. This is a tool that I am happy to pass on, although I am sure that people less dysfunctional than I probably do this instinctively.

This is from well-known graphic designer Milton Glaser: "There is a test to determine whether someone is toxic or nourishing in your relationship with them. Here is the test: You have spent some time with this person, either you have a drink or go for dinner or you go to a ball game.

"It doesn't matter very much but at the end of that time you observe whether you are more energized or less energized. Whether you are tired or whether you are exhilarated. If you are more tired, then you have been poisoned. If you have more energy you have been nourished."

So simple! Now imagine an afternoon with a zombie, or with my ex-husband Pretty Boy Boyd. Pretty exhausting, right? Especially the time with Boyd. I've also come across a quotation from Mark Twain which pretty much sums up Boyd's half of any given conversation. Ready? "I have been through some terrible things in my life, some of which actually happened."

Of course, there are also those people who give you a lot of energy, but it's the kind of energy you get after eating more than your share of Sue Ten's special double-fudge bourbon-pecan brownies with mocha frosting.

In both cases, the ascent is rapid and thrilling, but some time long after the arc of the evening reaches its zenith, you're likely to wake up alone in a ravine. I'm not saying that we expect you to be all smiles when you are here.

Lord, no. We have The Morning Guy's Stepford Girlfriend here for that, and she has done a wonderful job of giving happiness a bad name. She's in the next room now with her feather duster, singing the entire soundtrack from Mary Poppins. Personally, I find her a wee bit tiring, but she passes the not-toxic test for him, and that's what matters. Maybe when his current bout of exhilaration wears off, I can get him to fix the screen door on my cottage.

If you have your own test for toxicity—or for true friendship—let me know. Better yet, tell me how you deal with it. One of the regulars at the driving range always says her older sister's name before she hits the ball. "Margaret! Margaret! Margaret!" If no one else is around, she'll yell it right out loud.

Perhaps at The Slice of Heaven 24-Hour Pie Shop and Driving Range, we should set aside an hour from time to time and encourage more yelling like that. I think it might be an important community service.

For dessert, I'll serve some Anadama Pie, and I guarantee you'll want to come back for more.

In Hot Pursuit of Happiness

One of the many joys here at The Slice of Heaven 24-Hour Pie Shop and Driving Range is the weekly meeting of Swamp Talk, a discussion group whose members for the most part have not fully adapted themselves to life behind the gate house at Pancho Villas, our nearby "Over 55" community. Every Friday morning, we push a few tables together, set out a couple of pots of coffee, and leave them pretty much alone.

I join them whenever I can, and I am really looking forward to this week's topic: "How can we redesign the way we live?"

I'm curious to see what varieties of utopia arise from this discussion, and of course I am working on my own, reviewing some old ideas that I've stored somewhere in the cobwebby back room of my mind, remembering past workshops and novel-writing attempts.

For Swamp Talk, this topic arose from a discussion on energy sources, specifically natural gas. (Is it really clean? Or is it just another scam? I'm a little skeptical since most of the information I could find came from the natural gas companies and their thinly veiled lobbyists.) Now that I've had a little time to mull it over, though, I am looking at the challenge from another perspective.

What design for the way we live would generate the most happiness? Last year I read *The Geography of Bliss*, which was, simply put, great fun. Imagine a curmudgeon setting out to explore the countries said to be the tops in happiness. Take it from there.

My mother always told me, "Happiness isn't everything," and I have been pondering that for years. I think she meant to say "personal happiness" or "your own damn happiness" but she went for the full sweep. Maybe God felt that way, too, when he smote Sodom and Gomorrah. Were those people truly evil, or were they just having too much fun? The pictures in my Sunday School comics were difficult to interpret. If there were both evil-doers and victims, shouldn't God have saved the victims?

Anyway, Sodom and Gomorrah are not my model for a perfect world since I don't party all night and day, and I don't drink, except on vacation and during hurricanes.

My question for all-you-all today is: "What if we redesigned the way we live making our top criteria the highest possible happiness for the largest number of people?"

What would we get? Is that ever the top of the list for urban planners? I don't know, but I suspect they go for more mundane goals such as ease of transportation, optimal land use, access to health care, lifelong education, and art in the parks. I think I'll have all that in my redesigned world, too, but as means to an end, and the end will be . . . happiness.

Already, I'm looking at you, my dear friends, here at The Slice of Heaven 24-Hour Pie Shop and Driving Range, and I've got to say, for the most part you seem to be a fairly happy crew, except of course for Pretty Boy Boyd, but he would not be happy anywhere except possibly floating face down in a vat of Guinness.

The question is, how do we export our level of satisfaction out to the rest of the world? What do we have right here that makes us happy?

My first observation is that we have community. The layout is a little quirky. We have no central command center unless you count the bar over at The Swing Barn. We live in a variety of dwellings and situations, ranging from my modest turquoise conch cottage to Sue Ten's top-of-the-line double wide to the villas at Pancho Villas and, of course, the Clown Castle, and The Morning Guy's current abode at Stepford South. I'm not really sure where your second-cousin Darnell is living these days, but I sure hope he's moved out of my car. I may need to drive to the Village one day this week.

So, yes! Community. We have it. We care for each other, and we look out for each other. We think of ourselves as "us" and the rest of the world is "them." We are right, and they are wrong. Yes! Say it out loud. It feels good, doesn't it?

I'm not sure if that's an essential part of happiness, but the sense of rightness does help. What else do we have here? Meaningful employment, whether it's baking pies, restocking the soda machine, tracking the iguanas, or being the first one to pick up the microphone on Karaoke night.

We have universal health care, at least for minor emergencies. Nurse Crotchett made sure we all had our flu shots, we get plenty of exercise hitting golf balls and walking over to The Swing Barn or out to the phone booth by the highway. If any one is feeling a little sluggish, Sue Ten will offer to give him or her a little power boost from a potato clock, just for fun.

We are in harmony with nature, and a maybe just a little bit scared of it when we hear the bull gators call out. We understand that the home we have chosen tends to descend into chaos during hurricane season, and we do what we can to discourage further development of the swamp. We especially enjoy it when visiting engineers and government consultants come by for some pie and coffee.

As much as we love our traditions, we also love to try out something new whenever possible. Even now, Joe Sparkle Junior is hatching a scheme for faster pie delivery to

The Swing Barn. So far, it involves a lot of cable and pulleys, and I'm not sure he's fully thought it out, but I admire his initiative.

We don't worry too much about law-enforcement since we all keep a pretty good watch on each other. The Morning Guy has drawn up plans for some solar panels, mainly to keep the lights on so we can still use the driving range at night when the storms knock out the power lines. We don't really need much in the way of transportation since there are so few places we'd rather be.

Maybe the key to Utopia isn't designing to produce happiness after all. Maybe it's designing to bring out the best in the people who already live there, or in our case, here.

Let me know what you think. What would my world look like if you ruled it?

Why I Live at the Sand Trap

With apologies to Eudora Welty

You may call it a bunker.
I call it a beach.

An ironic oasis in a desert of green,
Its mission is clear,
its intent gives me pause:
a time for reflection,
a change of horizon.

My sand wedge in hand,
I fear not the descent.
I hit the sand,
propel the ball,
and I am out too soon
with hardly a chance
to fully imagine
a lifetime of sand
with striped umbrellas
and cool lemonade,
perhaps something stronger for you.

The Slice of Heaven

    I wouldn't mind
    a whole game played
    from bunker to bunker
    from dune to dune
    from beach to beach,
    transistor radio crackling out
    those songs of summers past.

    I know there's a river of cool
    below the surface, and
    I'm tempted to lurk
    like the troll 'neath that bridge
    waiting to see who'll pay for safe passage,
    who'll pay the toll:
    beach blankets, umbrellas, toy trucks,
    buckets, and scoops.

    From sand box to sand trap,
    it all feels like home.

    Yes, I'll move on for now,
    but I'm sure I'll be back

Muffins

Sue Ten has been talking about adding "muffins" to The Pie Shop menu lately, but I do think she is mistaken. Surely she means adding breakfast muffins to The *Swing Barn* menu for those few fools who think breakfast should be full of fluff and sweetness.

Wait a minute, that would be me. No, not really. I want breakfast to have bacon, toast, eggs, grits, and some sort of garnish, and maybe an nice twist of Florida orange. A muffin is an afternoon food, or perhaps really an accoutrement to the entree. It should be a bit grainy, and small.

I don't know where this current breakfast muffin craze came from. I think it's a little wacky, and I don't believe that what people are calling muffins today are muffins at all but are instead some sort of glorified cupcake.

I'm with Frank Zappa here, on the muffin question: "Now some people they like cupcakes . . . ." And why not? Especially the Hostess variety, chocolately with those white squiggles on top. Yum. I ate those for years, until the advent of Ding Dongs and Ring Dings. Oh, my teeth hurt just thinking about it.

And then there were the birthday cupcakes that we had one year for the twins—little cakes piled high with frosting beyond belief. For some reason, blue was the color of the day and the frosting was spread from child to sugarfied child quick as a wink or a wiggle.

Each cupcake had a little blue clown head with pointed cap; each child wore a pointed blue clown cap. All in all, a fairly eerie site. Good thing the whole crew was outside and we were just able to hose them down later on. What do parents of winter-birthday children do? I shudder to think.

Muffins, though, should be nourishing and life giving. I remember one particular camping trip in Maine, when my fellow drinkers, I mean partiers, no I mean campers, chided me for bringing along a dozen blueberry muffins from the Jordan Marsh bakery. Ah, but in the morning, when we opened our bleary eyes and spied that sadly maligned Jordan Marsh bakery box, my stock rose as fast as the sun. Yes, muffins can be nourishing and life giving.

Corn-meal muffins are the perfect accompaniment to fish chowder, and bran muffins are, well, medicinal at best. Banana nut muffins reek of tea time. Let's see, then there are all manner of poppy seed ones, lemon grass, and who knows what else.

Muffins are a step up from biscuits, and a stair case up from the nasty burned things that my mother called "bride's biscuit" decades after she was a bride.

So how did they become the trashy breakfast dessert things they are today? The monsters with umbrella-mushroom tops handing over the edge? I don't know.

I've also noticed that in some parts of the country people refer to donuts as "rolls" and I think calling near-cupcakes "muffins" is the same faux-healthiness. Oh, how can I eat something big and sweet and pretend that it's really good for me? I know. I'll call it a muffin. All 2,000 calories of it.

So, "No," to Sue Ten. The Slice of Heaven 24-Hour Pie Shop and Driving Range will not be adding muffins to the menu, but I will give you my recipe for corn muffins and you can serve them on Saturday nights along with the endless franks-and-beans buffet. Outside of that, steer clear.

We are a pie shop. And a driving range. Life is good.

Lemon Mirage Pie

I've been doing a little time traveling lately, and I am reporting back to say the trip was highly successful. I visited the Southwestern part of the great U.S. of A., circa 1976, and was surprised to discover that my high school sweetheart was living but a few miles away from me. Of course, in real time, I had no way of knowing that since I had not seen or heard from him since the summer of 1965.

"Why time travel?" you might well ask. "Don't you have enough to do at The Pie Shop and Driving Range without gallivanting around the time-space continuum? Aren't you worried that you might accidentally change history and miss out on all the friends and loved ones you have now?"

Well, no. I don't worry about that much at all. For one thing, I suspect that you are not that easy to lose.

For another, I enjoy the fantasy that we are happily coexisting in different configurations in alternate realities all the time anyway. I'm just especially attached to this particular reality where there are so many lessons yet for me to learn.

But back to the Southwest in the late 1970s: One of my favorite places there was the great dry lake, or playa, near Willcox, Arizona.

If you walk out on the cracked and dry land toward the center of the lake, you will at some point realize that you are surrounded by a 360-degree mirage. There, you can convince some fairly gullible people that you are now invisible and can do whatever you like.

Warning: You might want to try a few gullibility tests outside the mirage before attempting anything too elaborate. I loved the idea of living inside a mirage, a conceit which is itself a mirage, and so I wrote this poem, way back then:

NOTES ON LIVING INSIDE A MIRAGE . . . .
>
> They'll have to admit
> I've gotten harder to find.
> The illusion I'm here is proof enough.
> I no longer need guards posted outside
> to gain belief in my frail disguise.
> (A mad dog or two is enough.)
> I hold my mirage skin before me
> like a face held up only by bones.
> And those who love me,
> those I must trust
> prevent the world from consuming my life
> by keeping in touch with my wavering light.
> Passing by, they falter and halt,
> taking the chance of talking to air.
> They shout at the blur to reach me,
> but I'm wrapped like an island
> in that watery haze
> that cushions the landfall
> from the storm dreaming sea.
> In silence,
> I gauge their uncertain eyes,
> their every response
> whenever they think they've found my soul.
> And just as they leave me,
> they'll tell me one more time
> if this shimmering skin
> is just around me,
> or if it's wrapped around everything else.

That was the desert. Now back-flip me to Maine and my life at 16. It's a place and time I rarely visit, but now that I have made contact with my former true love, I've feel safe to unfurl those memories which I've left rolled up so tightly like scrolls for years. Or maybe more like one of those noise makers that you have to blow into to give dimension and sound.

I've enjoyed seeing myself as a optimistic girl again, and learning that she was intelligent, artsy, and quirky, all in a good way, mohair sweaters, white lipstick, and all. I'm still flicking the dust off some of those souvenir boxes, marveling always about how much was packed into such a small space of time.

Now, it seems, weeks go by with hardly a single significant event, and I remain the same. I grow a little more skilled at golf and pie-baking. I love you more all the time. I learn a new song for Karaoke night. I am happy, and yet dissatisfied. I've returned from time-traveling thinking I'm on the brink of something new, and maybe I am. Or maybe I just need to spend more time exploring mirages.

As The Pie Shop takes on an increasingly Victorian ambiance, perhaps we'll draw in a few steampunk deep-thinkers who will take multi-dimensional travel seriously, as they sit around and sip tea from bone china cups and savor my lemon-mirage pie.

Who knows? Maybe they'll be able to convince me that the road not taken does, in fact, go somewhere else. So far, I'm not so sure. After all, what road did you take to bring you here? Not the one that I took, but I'm always happy to see you walk in the door, still in your safari togs.

Yes, I've lived in the desert. I know what it's like to see it dry out until it cracks. I've lived in the mirage and dreamt of water night after night. We have no mirages in the swamp, but we do have golf and pie, and maybe that's enough.

The City

When Sue Ten asked if I wanted to spend a couple of days with her in the city, naturally I assumed she meant Miami and said "Sure!" As it turns out, she meant New York City, a place I had not visited, nor missed, for 30 years.

I have never made any secret of my bumpkinism. In Missouri, when I'd walk down the sidewalks of Kansas City with my ex-husband Pretty Boy Boyd, he would consistently and persistently tell me to stop smiling at people, saying "You're in the city now."

But, really, I couldn't help it, and for the most part, I never really believed that the city was much more than an illusion. Surely the buildings and traffic were just a temporary aberration, a mirage perhaps, and none of the trappings were meant to be a "lifestyle."

I simply couldn't recognize it as anything real, any more than the Arawak Indians could see the boats of Columbus. They knew there was something wrong with the water, of course, but caravels with sails? Not possible. (Then again, Columbus had his own vision problem and could not see the Arawak as human beings, either.)

To Sue Ten, though, the city is home, and it calls to her every bit as loudly as the bull gators call to me, out here on the edge of the 'Glades. No matter. I love to travel, and this city of hers turned out to be every bit as fascinatingly foreign to me as San Jose in Costa Rica or Hong Kong.

The sounds alone were a treat: We heard languages galore, and I made a recording of the subway so I can compare that sound file to the one I made of the BART in San Francisco.

We visited museums, met goddesses, saw the Gay Pride parade, toured historic landmarks, walked for miles, crossed bridges, listened to opera singers, paid $10 for four tiny meatballs, cheered on circus performers, declined to pay $10 for cotton candy, had a slice and a grape at Coney Island, viewed Frank Lloyd Wright's un-constructed masterpieces, and waited in line at the drug store, right behind a bearded lady.

My favorite part was sitting in green plastic lawn chairs in Times Square. The chairs were remarkably similar to the ones we set out for movie night at The Swing Barn, although I swear ours are in better condition, the plastic not yet fully shredded. The Morning Guy would never put up for that, not while there is still duct tape to be had somewhere on the planet.

Not unlike The Slice of Heaven 24-Hour Pie Shop and Driving Range, Times Square—at least at ground level—is now an oasis, surrounded by traffic and humanity. I'm pretty sure you can get pie there some where, but golf is probably frowned upon.

I do think they could put in a putting green, though. Of course, the traffic and humanity surrounding The Slice of Heaven has the good sense to keep a respectful distance.

I'm looking forward to going back to the city in another 30 years. By then, perhaps, Times Square will be a garden spot with fabulous water features and gigantic blossoming trees. As usual, I can't wait to see what will happen next.

Pretty Boy, by the way, is summering in the land of his own native asphalt, which gives all of the regulars at The Swing Barn a little chance to carry on their own conversations without having him skillfully change all their stories into less interesting ones about him. Just before he left, our new neighbor and local salsa-dance therapist,

Loretta Beauregard, analyzed Boy's salsa moves as ones that are only possible (or conceivable) for a full-blown narcissist.

Sue Ten told her that diagnosis didn't even require a degree from a school that advertises on match book covers. "What else do you call a man who likes to sit next to the Wurlitzer jukebox, not for the music but for the reflection?" she asked. "You ought to try analyzing someone a bit less obvious, like my husband Logan or my internet boyfriend Hector."

I'm never sure how much what's-left-of-Logan can hear from the back room, lit by the glow of CNN, so I changed the subject and asked Loretta how her salsa-therapy classes at Pancho Villas Over-55 Retirement Community and Golf Club was going.

"So far, it's just as you predicted," she said. "No one remembers anything from one week to the next, so we'll be on Lesson One for a long, long time."

"Perfect," I said. "Life is just as easy as you let it be."

Moon Landing

As you know, we are big fans of Big Science here at The Slice of Heaven 24-Hour Pie Shop and Driving Range, and what could be bigger, scientifically speaking, than putting a man or two on the moon?

After all, if Neil Armstrong, Buzz Aldrin, and Cmdr. Collins had not made that initial trip 40 years ago, our favorite astronaut Alan Shepard might never have been the first man to play golf on the lunar surface. For our Moon Landing celebration, we had plenty of Alan Shepard Pie, we listened to NASA's re-broadcast of the whole event, and we held a contest to solve the content-relevant puzzles in the *New York Times*.

We had a lot of moon songs on the juke box—"Blue Moon," "Moon Dance," and "Moon Shadow," to name a few—and Sue Ten showed *Moonstruck* on the side of The Swing Barn our usual lawn chair and popcorn crowd. Loretta Beauregard, the salsa-dance therapist, was on hand to give us all some lessons and some listening, and we thoroughly enjoyed ourselves.

I read recently that the computers used by mission control and on Apollo were perhaps as powerful as our cell phones, probably not as powerful as your own GPS golf-tracking systems, certainly not as sophisticated at the system that Sue Ten has set up at The Swing Barn to mash-up Karaoke renditions with key variables such as harmonic success, type of liquor sold during each song, and amount of money in her tip jar.

I've just got to wonder, though, if computers have become so much more clever, why isn't the space program growing at a faster rate. Where's my hover car? Shouldn't we all have a space-station vacation home by now? Shouldn't I be eating pie in zero-G and working on my short game on the lunar surface. I must say, I'm a tad disappointed.

Your second-cousin Darnell blames the robots, although he was a bit more colorful in his description of exactly what he calls a robot. He seems to think that the robots took all the good jobs, and left him with few options beyond becoming a greeter at Wal-Mart or a bag boy at Publix.

I'm not so sure. I don't know that I have ever actually met a robot, but I would like to. I do know that a lot of great technology—and I'm not just talking about Tang here—has come from the space program. Think of the medical advances alone. So, as we sat around with our slices of Alan Shepard pie and our glasses of Tang (I had some stored in the fall-out shelter), we talked about how we might personally benefit from more spin offs.

As you know by now, I plan to live to 120 for starters, so I want to believe that technology will help me out. I have no problem at all with cybernetic knees. I'm sure they are a good thing. Elbows, too. Maybe hips. Maybe more. And, in another 60 years, I might need even more parts. What about you? Where's the line for your own descent into robotology? I'd really like to know.

Taxi Driver

I have already told you about going to New York with Sue Ten, but a few weeks after *any* event involving her, I like to see what parts of the story will rise to the top, like cream ready to be skimmed out of a bottle of farm-fresh milk.

Now, seriously, I am not a city person by any stretch of imagination. I get rattled in crowds that are not headed to or from a ballgame. I hear too many heart beats around me, and I don't know how to shut them out. I'm too busy gawking to watch where I am going, and I feel like I am constantly trying to break through the surface of ice on a pond to find a more familiar horizon.

So why go to New York with Sue? Ah, well. Pretty easy answer: She asked me, and she also said, "Do you like to plan your trips?" Oh, my. Magic words. In no time at all I had a website set up; an interactive calendar in place; and a spreadsheet of what, when, and where all worked out.

"Oh," she said. But of course, she already knew all that about me. After all, geekiness is something hard to hide for long, although it is more and more commonly accepted today as "normal" especially by people who don't know the origin of the term. Geek, my dear, is really a type of carney folk who specialize in odd things like biting heads off lizards, and other acts of dismemberment and displaced body parts.

Geeks will fry frogs alive and pop them in their mouths. Geeks will follow up the frog trick by popping out their own eyeballs and eating them, too.

There's really no limit to geekdom, and I do promise you, I try to keep that kind of geek out of The Pie Shop kitchen, although they do pretty well on the driving range since what they lack in skill they make up with creativity.

And so it goes.

Yes, we made our plan, and I do love a plan—even a hasty, ill-conceived one—and we followed it through and through. I think Sue's favorite part, at least in the re-telling, was to call a car service to take us to the airport to fly home.

That went well until the neophyte taxi driver tried to kidnap us, or so it seemed. I, of course, was a total innocent, just going along for the ride, confident that transporttion in The City would be every bit as reliable as it is at home when whoever happens to be the designated driver for the day sets out with his or her precious cargo.

Boy oh boy, was I mistaken. This guy had no apparent idea about where he was going but he was determined to take us there anyway. We knew we were in trouble when, soon after we had settled into the Town Car, Sue answered her phone, and it was the dispatcher saying "He'll be right there."

"Right where? We're in the car."

"Are you in a black car?"

"No, we're in a gray car."

Okay, that was bad, but optimism reigned. One cab, two cabs, how different could they be? And then he took the wrong exit, and Sue started to quiz him. Or interrogate him. Or get into his face, which was difficult from the back seat since Sue did not want to take her seatbelt off.

Then she started yelling at me to call 9-1-1, which made no sense to me at all since I knew my phone would call the local Everglades dispatch and what good would that do me in New York City.

Sue later told me I'd just have to tell them where we were. "But I didn't know where we were!" Even now, she is incredulous remembering my face as I handed her the phone.

Oh, Good Lord. What would I have done without her? Would I have been sold into white slavery? Or was that Japanese businessman who took a liking to me in China behind the whole escapade? I don't know. Somehow Sue gained command of the episode, and she convinced the driver to follow her instructions to the letter, and we did—sure enough—end up at LaGuardia airport in plenty of time for our flight to SoFLA.

And now, can you believe it, I'm about to go to New York again, and it hasn't even been six months, not to mention 30 years. This time I'm on a mission with the American Pie Council to attend the Martha Stewart Pie Special. I'm totally cracking up about the whole thing, and am still working on my pie design. Some sort of poetry pie, I think. Maybe a brownie pie with a ginger snap crust, the poems tucked into foil doilies between the slices. I am psyched.

And I have no intention of getting into a New York City cab with Sue Ten.

The Slice of Heaven

Pie Poems for the Poetry Pie

Oh trouble trouble trouble. What shall I bake for the Martha Stewart pie show? I had such grandiose ideas of different ways to create a poetry pie, but let's face it, we're flying 1,500 miles to get there, and it's going to be tough enough to get my pie with its silver doilies through TSA, although I did check the website and they claim there really is no problem at all.

I'll just send it through the X-ray machine and be on my way, flying to NYC with a pie on my lap, my Mohawk friend Hannah next to me all the way. Believe me, we are some excited. I've decided: The pie, my dears, will be a decadent brownie pie with a ginger snap crust. Gooey and spicy. Pretty I hope. I make the practice pie tonight, I think.

But first it needs to be crammed with poetry, just like McCabe (in the Altman film *McCabe and Mrs. Miller*). And the poetry needs to be of the postcard variety, only about pies and baking, not trains this time.

PAT'S APPLE RAISIN PIE
Kayaking in Florida's 10,000 islands,
expeditioning with Outward Bound,
I finally shed one more food phobia
and ate a meal that included raisins—
didn't even try to pick them out.
But still, you know, even so, I don't regret
passing up Pat's Apple Pie with Rum-Soaked Raisins
in the filling. It just did not seem right
there on the table with our stoic New England fare.

Yogurt Dream Pie

Yogurt! I loved it! Made it myself in funny
little cups, plugged into a yellow warming tray that
I bought from some catalog. I put it in
everything, even Dream Whip pie with lemon
Jello-O and who knows what else. "I like it,"
said Dad, pointing with his fork. "What's in it?"
"Yogurt," I beamed, then watched in astonishment
as he pushed it way, slid back his chair, and
left the kitchen for the comfort and security
of his old, familiar recliner.

Steak and Mushroom Pie

We bought the first one in a tin in some tiny
gourmet shop in Portland, Maine, so cool we were
as college students, English majors, worldly
in our willingness to try something new, something
that I could replicate in our galley kitchen where I had
Already failed so stupendously to create *coq au vin*
and had come up with pink chicken. But, my dear,
let me tell you, that steak and mushroom pie, the
one that I made myself, still sizzles on my tongue, leaving
its savory essence in memory ever better, every year.

Mincemeat Pie

"Mincemeat pie," I said to John, "was invented by Paul Bunyan
after Babe the Blue Ox finished off the last of the
real minces, a single-ox extermination unit, that one. So
Paul had to create a dish every bit as sweet and delicious.
I don't know whether he poured brandy into the first
one, or if that was someone else's idea, so in either case,
what you have here is actually mock mince.
Not mince."

"Can't say that I care," he said, and sliced his way
through my crust of cookie-cuttered stars, ate his way
into yet another Great American Myth.

Another Thanksgiving, Another Pie
Somehow, my son and I developed our
own tradition over the years, never quite getting
the pumpkin pie right, always managing to forget
one ingredient, never two, always finagling our
way through the shopping list, then opening the
oven door to find something unexpected in
shape or texture, but always finding something
for sure that we could pass off as pie.

Boston Cream in Boston
When Nanny turned 72, we all hauled down to
Boston for a night at The Pops, preceded by a
dinner at Jakey Wirth, me a satellite to Nanny's family
who gossiped and sipped, drank beer,
drank wine. And for dessert the crisp waiters trouped
out with the most fabulous Boston Cream Pie
I have seen in my life, decadent as only custard
and chocolate can be. She cut us each an
ample slice, and surveyed her congenial tribe with
a nod and a knowing grin, a bit of custard on her lip.

The Line

I just had an excellent night out on the range with Nurse Crotchett. She's made an outstanding discovery that we both play so much better than normal if we use orange tees. Apparently, it also helps if we wear similar, although not matching, outfits. Pink and white, preferably.

"Golf is so complicated!" she says. "No wonder more people don't play it." Crotchett is learning to play primarily through observation, especially when we have a certain species of athletic male on site.

I've known her to pull up a chair under the awning and spend several hours just soaking up skill sets as she sips on her iced coffee and slowly, deliberately finishes off another slice of mango crumb pie.

For myself, I've discovered that I can do my morning walk/run better if I sing "Benny & the Jets"—at least the small bit that I know—during the running part. I tend to go non-verbal during the walking part. Yes, we are all about accommodations here, learning what we can do to become more physically fit without letting our brains know what we are plotting.

While some people may preach a mind/body wholeness integrated spirituality and physical health system, we go more for a one-thing-a-time program. That's why Sue Ten never ever has a buffet at The Swing Barn. She just doesn't like the looks of all that slippage on a dinner plate.

There are, of course, limits. For example, apple pie and cheese is fine. Maybe even apple pie, cheese, and vanilla ice cream. But something goes awry with a fourth ingredient, and the whole thing needs to be marked FAIL with a fifth.

I'll agree that pizza, soups, and stews work out all right with multiple ingredients, but so many other dishes do not, and my question for you today is "Why?"

Yes, I know, that is usually my question. Perhaps I am a newly verbal toddler at heart. So let's make it a bit more refined. Where's the line?

If Crotchett and I look great in our coordinated outfits, and play better golf, wouldn't we play even more expertly if we looked completely alike, similar perhaps to the Fem-Bots who visited us last Halloween? Apparently not. We've tried it.

At what point does pie go from perfect to fail?

When does too much of a good thing go from being just right to not enough?

Where's the line?

Some people, like The Morning Guy, seem to have excellent radar for The Line, no matter what they are doing in life. I usually don't know it's there until I've tripped over it. And your second-cousin Darnell is pretty much always on the other side of it completely.

I guess I will just add "line vision" to the list of super powers I wish I had. First, if you recall, I wish I had the power to always ask the right question. Let's face it. Usually I don't ask any questions, I just plunge into the depths and deal with regrets later on.

Today, though, I want to be able to see The Line. What will that do for me? I don't know. Still, if I ever ask you, "Do you see that, too?" I hope you'll know what I mean.

Ethan Coen's Poem

The other night, driving home from The Village and listening to NPR, I heard a wonderful interview with Ethan Coen, closed out by the actor William Macy reading one of the poems.

"The drunken driver has the right of way," is the title of the poem, and toward the end of it, Coen notes, "When facing an oncoming fool / The practiced and sagacious say / Watch out / one side / look sharp / gang way."

That line stopped me short with its uncanny familiarity. After all, I've seen an oncoming fool or two in my time, and I'm sad to say it never dawned on me to step aside. For all of my study of *The Worst Case Scenario Handbook*, I still can't say that I have the sense to roll off a speeding sled before it hits a tree, a wall, a door.

Faced with an oncoming fool, I'm still likely to stand there like your typical deer in the headlights. After all, what is more likely to shake up my life than pure foolishness?

I know I have welcomed foolishness more often than not with open arms, leaving no one to blame but myself when the smoke finally clears and suddenly it is time to sift through the saw dust on the floor to identify the bullet casings.

In many ways, Coen's poem reminds me of both of my ex-husbands, Patrick the Liar and Pretty Boy Boyd. They were and are still, I'm sure, masters at getting their way, often by creating a massive presence so wildly unstable that sharper souls than I can *easily* recognize its foolishness by the undulations alone, and stand clear.

The Slice of Heaven

Until now, at least, I've lacked the energy to remain vigilant, especially when I was never really sure whether that careening vehicle headed down my lane was evidence of an alert driver dodging raccoons—or a drunk driver navigating entirely by the sound of the gravel road against his tires.

I get tired just thinking about those days, yet think about them I do, preferably from the haven of the front porch of my turquoise conch cottage here on the edge of the 'Glades, just out of sight of The Slice of Heaven 24-Hour Pie Shop and Driving Range. Sue Ten and my other friends here are great anti-fool detectors, and I know I am safe with them nearby.

Even now, I can hear "Walk Like an Egyptian" playing on the distant jukebox, so I know The Morning Guy has flung open The Pie Shop windows, and soon he'll be punching in the numbers to play some Crosby, Stills, Nash, and Young.

Prentiss, my pie apprentice, has already served up her latest confection and gotten rave reviews. Joe Sparkle Junior is fussing around the new putting green, replacing the divots that The Clown and her pals kicked up during the night. It's an excellent day, just getting started with no drunken drivers in sight.

Untensed, I return to Coen's poem, and my reverie, thinking how some time ago, I read an English-to-Chinese-to-English translation of a quotation attributed to Mother Theresa. It was finally rendered as "The opposite of love is not hate. It is carelessness."

I've thought about that for a long time, and have never been able to shake the odd truth of it. Perhaps "apathy" was the word that the writer—or translator—sought, but "carelessness" makes more sense to me. The drunken driver is careless, from the moment he or she says, "Set 'em up, Joe." I prefer a life that is careful, or at least full of caring.

Let us not be careless, my dear friends. And now, I must warn you, I feel a country song coming on, a song about being careless. I don't know the tune, but here are the words:

> You threw the white silk nightie of my love
> into soapy hot water
> with your red-flannel heart
> and ruined them both.
>
> You took my long-playing records
> and left them to melt
> on the steam radiator of your disregard.
>
> You said you had no secrets
> and left a trail of credit-card carbons
> all the way to the motel door.
>
> You left me waiting at the butcher shop
> while you had bratwust at the bar.
>
> You were careless with my car
> and careless with my love
> but there's no no-fault insurance
> for what you have done.

Obviously this song still needs a little work, so perhaps I'll get back to that and polish it up before Sue Ten says it's time for another meeting of the Tone Deaf Choir next door at The Swing Barn. I think she'll like it when I am done, and maybe you will, too. Drop by soon. We've missed you.

The Winds of Insomnia

For the third time in as many days, I've awakened too early, vibrating with exhaustion. I thought when I exorcised my ex-husband Pretty Boy Boyd from my life, I would be facing a stress-free future, but nature hates a void, and the stress has rolled back in.

In this case, the stress is the result of that peculiar promise, "No good deed goes unpunished," and my punishment seems far more severe than my good deeds. Ah, well.

In many ways the stress has been almost nostalgic, familiar. In other ways, it has been the enemy, sneaking in through the back screen door, having taken special care to oil the hinges and drug the cat.

So, this morning, as I walked up the lane from my turquoise conch cottage to hit golf balls at 5:00 a.m., I was glad to hear Credence Clearwater Revival drifting down from the jukebox.

Since The Morning Guy was playing the jukebox, I knew he must be in a good mood, the soda machine must be fully restocked, and Prentiss The Pie Apprentice must have done well on her algebra exam.

I saw them both, sitting at opposite ends of the counter, bathed in the yellow glow of our faux gaslights, and I immediately relaxed, thinking some honeydew-yogurt dream pie would taste good, wishing I still drank coffee, and kissing stress good-bye at the door.

Friends, that is the magic of The Slice of Heaven 24-Hour Pie Shop and Driving Range, and how I've missed spending more time with you there. That, my dears, is the greatest antidote to stress that I know.

I was not the only one with her hair blown back by the winds of insomnia this morning either. Nurse Crotchett was already on the putting green, working her way out to longer and longer putts. Soon she'll be at three feet, and then who knows what new challenges she will attempt.

I would love to have more customers like Crotchett. She pays her $10 for all the balls she can hit, but makes each effort such a study in preparation, she sometimes does not hit more than 10 in the same time that it takes me to hit 90. She certainly saves us a lot of wear and tear on the balls.

The sun is coming up and soon it will be time to read the headlines to your second-cousin Darnell. No, he's not illiterate, but he did take the "What kind of learner are you?" quiz on Facebook, and now refuses to read since he's audio-oriented and reading would be a waste of his precious time. (I, on the other hand, just refuse to take quizzes on Facebook.)

Perhaps tonight I will sleep. Perhaps I'll dream of you and see your wonderful smile. For now though, I'll just enjoy the pale light brightening around me, here at the little pie shop on the edge of the 'Glades.

The Slice of Heaven

www.ingramcontent.com/pod-product-compliance
Lightning Source LLC
Chambersburg PA
CBHW051648040426
42446CB00009B/1038